HISTORY OF THE INSURRECTIONS
IN MASSACHUSETTS IN 1786

A Da Capo Press Reprint Series

THE ERA OF THE AMERICAN REVOLUTION

GENERAL EDITOR: LEONARD W. LEVY

Claremont Graduate School

HISTORY OF THE
INSURRECTIONS IN
MASSACHUSETTS IN 1786
AND OF THE REBELLION
CONSEQUENT THEREON

By George Richards Minot

DA CAPO PRESS · NEW YORK · 1971

A Da Capo Press Reprint Edition

This Da Capo Press edition of *History of the Insurrections in
Massachusetts in 1786...*, is an unabridged republication of the
first edition published in Worcester, Massachusetts, in 1788. It is
reprinted by permission from a copy of the original edition in the
Enoch Pratt Free Library, Baltimore, Maryland.

Library of Congress Catalog Card Number 76-148912
SBN 306-70100-6

Published by Da Capo Press
A Division of Plenum Publishing Corporation
227 West 17th Street, New York, N.Y. 10011

Manufactured in the United States of America

HISTORY OF THE INSURRECTIONS
IN MASSACHUSETTS IN 1786

THE

HISTORY

OF THE

INSURRECTIONS,

IN

MASSACHUSETTS,

In the YEAR MDCCLXXXVI,

AND THE

REBELLION

CONSEQUENT THEREON.

BY GEORGE RICHARDS MINOT, A. M.

PRINTED AT *WORCESTER*, MASSACHUSETTS,
BY ISAIAH THOMAS. MDCCLXXXVIII.

PREFACE.

HOWEVER diſagreeable it may be to review the troubles of our country, every patriot will look upon it as his duty, not to let them paſs without notice. The period of misfortune is the moſt fruitful ſource of inſtruction. By inveſtigating the cauſes of national commotions, by tracing their progreſs, and by carefully marking the means through which they are brought to a concluſion, well eſtabliſhed principles may be deduced, for preſerving the future tranquillity of the Commonwealth. No perſon therefore, will conſider it as an unneceſſary renewal of painful ideas, or as a wanton publication of tranſactions, which ſome may wiſh, what indeed is impoſſible, to bury in oblivion, when we candidly and reſpectfully look into the late inſurrections. By ſuch a reſearch many miſconceived ideas, tending to the diſcredit of the country, may be removed ; and the publick reputation vindicated ; as the cauſes which led to the

late

late national difficulties, when rightly un-
derſtood, operate as an apology for them ;
and the manner in which theſe difficulties
were ſuppreſſed, does honour to the government, and diſplays the ſtrongeſt marks
of reflection and wiſdom in the people.

THE preſent time is thought the moſt
ſuitable for the following hiſtory, becauſe
the materials are moſt eaſily collected, and
any errours which may take place moſt
readily aſcertained, whilſt the events are recent. In ſome countries, ſtrong reaſons
might operate, for leaving it to poſterity,
to diſcover facts, under the diſadvantages of
diſtance of time, and the falſe impreſſions
perhaps, of imperfect tradition : But, from
the happy condition of our country, this duty may be performed at an earlier, and more
favourable ſeaſon. The ſpirit of party has
yielded to ſyſtems of conciliation ; freedom
of inquiry, and the privilege of forming
opinions for ourſelves, are unreſtricted ; and
whilſt we preſerve decency of expreſſion,
there is neither a diſpoſition in our magiſ-
trates, nor any authority known in our
laws, to ſilence or control the language of
truth. HISTORY

HISTORY

OF THE

INSURRECTIONS, &c.

I N

MASSACHUSETTS, in MDCCLXXXVI.

PART I.

 N order to judge rightly of the caufes which led to the infurrections in *Maffachufetts*, in the year 1786, and the unfortunate rebellion which enfued, it will be neceffary to take a view of the fituation of that Commonwealth at the clofe of the war. The citizens were then left free·indeed, and in full poffeffion of the valuable objects which they had fought

to obtain. But the price of thofe objects was high, and could not but be attended with the ufual confequences of great exertions, when founded on the anticipation of publick refources. Their private ftate debt, when confolidated, amounted to upwards 1,300,000 l. befides 250,000 l. due to the officers and foldiers of their line of the army. Their proportion of the federal debt, was not lefs, by a moderate compution, than one million and an half of the fame money. And, in addition to this, every town was embarraffed, by advances which they had made, to comply with repeated requifitions for men, and fupplies to fupport the army, and which had been done upon their own particular credit. The weight of this burden muft ftrike us in a ftrong point of view, if we compare it with the debt before the war, which fell fhort of 100,000 l. and with ftill more force, perhaps, if we confider, that by the cuftomary mode of taxation, one third part of the whole was to be paid by the rateable polls alone, which but little exceeded ninety thoufand. True it is, that a recollection of the bleffings which this debt had purchafed, muft have operated, in the minds of a magnanimous people, to alleviate every inconvenience arifing from fuch a caufe; but embarraffments followed which no confiderations of that nature could be expected to obviate.

UPON

UPON the right management then, of the publick debt, the future tranquillity of the Commonwealth greatly depended : And it was a melancholy circumftance, that various caufes exifted to
prevent a fair experiment of the abilities of the
people to difcharge it. They had been laudably
employed, during the nine years in which this
debt had been accumulating, in the defence of
their liberties ; but, though their conteft had in-
ftructed them in the nobler fcience of the rights
of mankind, yet it gave them no proportionable
infight into the mazes of finance. Their honeft
prejudices were averfe from duties of impoft and
excife, which were, at that time, fuppofed to be
antirepublican by many judicious and influential
characters. Thefe meafures, therefore, could be
adopted, at firft, but partially, and to fmall effect.
The neceffary arrangements at the treafury were
wanting. The paper currency was failing, and,
though from the great and complete exertions of
Maffachufetts to redeem her proportion of the
continental bills of credit, *their* decay muft have
affected her faith as little as that of any ftate in
the union, yet confequences of this expiring medium could not be unfelt. Under fo many dif-
couraging circumftances, it was not, perhaps,
within the compafs of human power, to refcue
the

the publick credit, on which the means of happiness in every community so essentially depend.

SUCH disposition of this debt, however, was made as the situation of things would admit. Compliance was at length had with the resolution of Congress, for laying an impost duty of five per centum, for the purpose of paying the foreign debt ; and an impost and excise was adopted for discharging the interest of the debt of the Commonwealth. But these measures could reduce the tax upon polls and estates, at that time, in a small degree only. The former expedient could not come into effect till the other states had adopted it ; and the produce of the latter was not equal to its appropriation. Much of the burden was, therefore, left to the old mode of taxation, annually reminding the people of a pressure, which the change of their manners by the war had made them less able to bear.

WITH these embarrassments one would suppose, that the highest object which could have been aimed at, would have been to provide for the punctual payment of the interest of the national debt. Yet either the impatience of the people at paying interest money, which was compared to a canker worm that consumed their substance without lessening their burdens, or some other cause,

                                    induced

induced the legiſlature, ſo early as the year 1784, to iſſue a tax of 140,000 l. for redeeming that amount of the army debt ; and in two years afterwards 100,000 l. more was aſſeſſed for the ſame purpoſe. The payment of the extant taxes was ſoon found to be much in arrear, notwithſtanding the depreciation of the certificates which were made receivable for them ; and, after ſtrict ſcrutiny into the conduct of publick officers employed in the collection, the delinquency was perceived to be in a great degree, with the people themſelves, from unavoidable cauſes.

THE conſequences of the publick debt did not firſt appear among the citizens at large. The bulk of mankind are too much engaged in private concerns to anticipate the operation of national cauſes. But the members of the legiſlature, poſſeſſed of information, and led by the duties of their office to attend to this debt, were early thrown into diviſions from the proſpect of the burdens which it preſented. The men of landed intereſt ſoon began to ſpeak plainly againſt trade, as the ſource of luxury, and the cauſe of loſing the circulating medium. The vices and indolence of the people were aſcribed to its inſtrumentality. This was urged as a reaſon that the taxes ſhould be thrown liberally upon commerce,

merce, fince, if it fupported them, the Commonwealth would be eafed ; and if it failed under the
weight, they would be rid of fo great a caufe of
political evil. From fuch fentiments the prejudices againft impoft and excife duties began to
give way, and fyftems were propofed, upon the
oppofite extreme, for raifing the whole revenue of
government by this now favourite mode of taxation. Commercial men, on the other hand, defended themfelves by infifting that the fault was
only in the regulations which the trade happened
to be under. To deftroy commerce would not
leffen the multitude of evils afcribed to its means ;
thefe would be introduced through the channel
of neighbouring ftates, and the reafonable advantages which might be derived from it, would be
thrown into their hands. Trade and agriculture,
they faid, were mutually beneficial to each other,
and ought to be equally partners in fupporting
the publick burden.

A DISTINCTION of interefts, on which the ap-
portionment of the national debt might fo much
depend, when once eftablifhed, was not afterwards fuffered to fubfide. It led to a divifion
upon all queftions of taxation, and even upon
other fubjects where it was fuppofed the ftrength
of thefe parties could be tried. When favourite

points

points were loft in thefe divifions, it gave a difguft to members in the minority, which was extended to other meafures, and, in fome inftances,
no doubt, biaffed their opinions, and mifguided
their influence, in the fphere of domeftick life.

IT muft be reckoned among the misfortunes of
the Commonwealth, that, when fo great burdens
were to be apportioned upon the people, the rule
in ufe fhould be liable to the objections of all parties, from the uncertainty of reducing it into equal
practice. Where a duty is enjoined with which
compliance is made, at beft, with reluctance, if
the leaft grounds are afforded for the mind to fuf-
pect injuftice or miftake, it produces pofitive dif-
obedience. The fhare of publick requifitions
fhould be affixed to property, by a known, un-
changing, and if poffible, a proportionate ftandard.
It then becomes involved in the value of the property, and that value is not afterwards fubject to
fluctuate from principles of taxation. The pof-
feffour is never furprifed with a weight of taxes beyond his calculation, nor exempted from his due
proportion at the expenfe of his neighbours. But,
whether fuch a rule can be unalterably eftablifhed
in a young country, where new property is daily
rifing into view, and the old changing in its value,
it may be difficult to determine. Certain it is,
however,

however, that, in forming a valuation in the year 1785, great, though not unusual, difficulties arose. Among other counties, those of *Hampshire* and *Berkshire* were said, by their members, to have been valued too high ; and some discontent must be attributed to this real or supposed errour.

THE usual consequences of war, were conspicuous upon the habits of the people of *Massachusetts*. Those of the maritime towns relapsed into the voluptuousness which arises from the precarious wealth of naval adventurers. An emulation prevailed among men of fortune, to exceed each other in the full display of their riches. This was imitated among the less opulent classes of citizens, and drew them off from those principles of diligence and economy, which constitute the best support of all governments, and particularly of the republican—Besides which, what was most to be lamented, the discipline and manners of the army had vitiated the taste, and relaxed the industry of the yeomen. In this disposition of the people to indulge the use of luxuries, and in the exhausted state of the country, the merchants saw a market for foreign manufactures. The political character of *America* standing in a respectable view abroad, gave a confidence and credit to individual citizens heretofore unknown. This credit was improved, and goods were imported to a

much

much greater amount, than could be confumed, or paid for. The evils of this excefs of importation were greatly aggravated, by the decayed condition of the commerce, and the little attention which had been paid during the war, to raifing of articles for exports. The fifheries, which may be called the mines of *Maffachufetts*, had been neglected, or but feebly improved, from the want of fhipping and other caufes. The whale fifhery, which from trifling beginnings in the year 1701, at length brought into the late Province, no lefs a fum than 167,000l. fterling, annually, through the ifland of *Nantucket* alone, and which employed 150 fail of veffels, with near 2500 feamen, was, at the opening of the peace, reduced to be the object of nineteen fail only. A great, if not a proportionable diminution, was vifible in other articles of exportation. In addition to this, what few could be obtained, were rendered almoft ufelefs, by one of the fevereft effects of the revolution— the lofs of many markets to which Americans had formerly reforted with their produce. Thus was the ufual means of remittance by articles of the growth of the country, almoft annihilated, and little elfe than fpecie remained, to anfwer the demands incurred by importations. The money, of courfe, was drawn off ; and this being inadequate

to

to the purpofe of difcharging the whole amount
of foreign contracts, the refidue was chiefly funk
by the bankruptcies of the importers. The fcarcity of fpecie, arifing principally from this caufe,
was attended with evident confequences; it checked commercial intercourfe throughout the community, and furnifhed reluctant debtors with an
apology for withholding their dues both from individuals and the publick.

ANOTHER effect of the war which was exceedingly operative in the commotions that took place
in *Maffachufetts*, if it may not be called their
primary caufe, was the accumulation of private
debts. The confufion of the times had excufed
or prevented moft perfons from difcharging their
contracts. Some indeed availed themfelves of an
advantage, which the laws of the country, for a
long time, put into their hands, and paid their
creditors in a depreciated currency ; and fome
might have difcharged their obligations in a more
honourable manner : But great part of the community were yet loaded with ancient debts, made
ftill more burdenfome from an increafe of intereft.
Private contracts were firft made to give place to
the payment of publick taxes, from an idea that the
fcarcity of fpecie did not admit of the payment
of both. The former therefore, were made pay-
able

able in other property than money, by an act of the 3d of *July*, 1782, commonly known by the name of the Tender Act. By this it was provided that executions issued for private demands might be satisfied by neat cattle and other articles particularly enumerated, at an appraisement of impartial men under oath. This act was obnoxious both to constitutional and equitable objections; but the necessity of the case overruled them all in the opinion of a majority in the government. The operation of the act was not altogether coincident with the ideas of its patrons. Its chief effect was to suspend lawsuits, which, by delaying, only strengthened and enlarged the evil when the year's existence of the law expired. But there was a circumstance which sprung out of this measure, infinitely more detrimental than any burden that it was intended to remove. It was the first signal for hostilities between creditors and debtors, between the rich and the poor, between the few and the many. It was by this act that the citizens of *Massachusetts*, experienced, that retrospective laws were not a violation of their boasted constitution, in the opinion of their legislature; and the multitude of debtors first felt from it, at an hour when their perplexities might lead them to an undue use of any advantage, that their
creditors

creditors were under their control. This principle rapidly increafed, and pretences fprung out of it, in many inftances, for ftopping the execution of law in private cafes, and, at length, for the bolder attack upon the courts themfelves.

IT muft be acknowledged that the time when this law made its appearance, was critical. Infurrections had happened in the county of *Hampfhire*, for the purpofe of oppofing both the Supreme Judicial Court, and the Court of Common Pleas at *Northampton*, in the month of *April* preceding ; a circumftance which feemed to operate both againft and in favour of the act. On the one hand, the motions of the people were confidered as evidence of their being oppreffed, and demonftrated the neceffity of alleviating meafures: On the other, there was great danger of facrificing to the complaints of a faction, what fhould be yielded only to the unqueftionable voice of the community. Whenever difcontent becomes the only condition of indulgence among any people, they cannot be happy, and, leaft of all, a people fituated as thofe of *Maffachufetts* were, at this fingular period. They were juft about quitting a well fought conteft, in which almoft every man had perfonally affifted. The applaufe of the world was frefh on their minds, and they felt a
title

title to retirement and repofe. Whatever interrupted this right, naturally appeared like a grievance, and became difcountenanced as an abridg-
ment of their liberties. They could not realize
that they had fhed their blood in the field, to be
worn out with burdenfome taxes at home ; or that
they had contended, to fecure to their creditors, a
right to drag them into courts and prifons.

WITH fuch high wrought notions of freedom
in the people, it was difficult for the legiflature
either to govern without appearing to tyrannife,
or to relieve without appearing to be overcome.
The General Court, in this dilemma, chofe to
confider the commotions of the populace, as evidence of their real diftreffes. And in addition to
the tender act, they paffed a law in the month of
November following, by which, with the indulgence of natural parents, they pardoned the rioters without a fingle exception.

THE fentiments entertained refpecting private
creditors could not long fail of reaching thofe of
the publick. The firft of this clafs of men who
fell under popular cenfure were the unfortunate
officers of the army. At a time when the country was difheartened with the appearance of an
unequal ftruggle, Congrefs thought it neceffary

B   to

to promife half pay for life to fuch of them as
would continue in fervice. This meafure occafioned no difficulties at the time, but when a
commutation of five years full pay, was given
them for this half pay, by a refolve of the 22d of
March 1782, though calculated upon principles
extremely favourable to the ftates, it raifed a general outcry ; and occafioned a tardinefs in the
payment of taxes. So great was the influence of
this clamour over the Houfe of Reprefentatives,
that they, for a long time, infifted upon introducing a claufe into a bill, then about to be paffed,
for granting an impoft to the *United States*, to
provide that no part of the proceeds of that duty,
from any of the ftates, fhould be applied to the
fulfilment of this advantageous contract.

THE cenfure of the people ought to have been,
and poffibly was leffened by a mortifying circumftance, on the part of the officers, arifing from the
very execution of this agreement. The addition
made to the federal domeftick debt, by their fecurities, which amounted to five million of dol-
lars, tended, with other caufes, to depreciate the
publick credit to fuch a degree, as that the current price of their notes would not make good
their eftablifhed pay, for the time they were in
actual fervice. But, if the difguft of the people
was

was in any degree diverted from the officers, it certainly did not quit any of the measures adopted for their pay. It was only transferred to such persons as had purchased their securities, and to the rest of the publick creditors. Through the want of confidence in the faith of government, these purchases had been made at a great discount. It soon became a common observation, that the promise of government could not, in equity, be extended to the man who was possessed of publick notes for a partial consideration, to intitle him to the payment of more than he gave; and that the legislature ought to avail themselves of the depreciation for the benefit of the Commonwealth. This principle was at length, reduced to system, and held up to the publick in print. When it was mentioned in the Representatives Chamber, an honest member asked, Whether the government had received any powers from the distressed creditors, who lost the difference between the real and nominal value of the notes, to detain the discount? Or, if they should detain it, Whether they designed to do so, for the purpose of restoring it to the original holders of the notes, to whom, in such case, it must undoubtedly belong? But this question was never answered.

B 2

FROM speculators in the funds, the cry of the discontented spread to original and indisputable creditors, of whom the consideration was immediately received by the publick. These indeed could not be denied their demands, but great fault was found with paying their interest money out of the impost and excise revenues, which was the most productive source of the government. At the reviving of these revenue laws in the session of *May* 1786, the appropriation of the proceeds of the duties, could not be carried agreeably to the former principles, but on condition of being subject to a revisal at the next assembling of the General Court, when, we shall find, one third part was appropriated to the exigencies of government.

THE numerous embarrassments under which the Commonwealth laboured soon after the war, produced a variety of expedients from the citizens. Among others, that which has been a peculiar favourite with the people of *America*, a paper money system, might well be expected to arise. Like their ancestors, the inhabitants of *Massachusetts* had, by they knew not what means, struggled through a variety of difficulties, with the aid of ideal wealth ; and, upon the appearance of new troubles, they felt inclined to revert to the same assistance.

affiftance. The injuftice and extreme diftrefs which had happened among individuals, and the burdens yet exifting on the Commonwealth, as a member of the union, from bills of credit, began to be effaced by the fuperiour objects which, it was thought, they had brought about. The revolution was afcribed to the powers of paper money, and it was held up as the price of every man's freedom. The propofition, however, was the lefs expedient, as great quantities of this currency in fact exifted and were circulating in the Commonwealth at the very time it was made. The delinquency in the payment of taxes had neceffitated the Treafurer to anticipate them, by orders on the Collectors. Thefe orders accumulating in a great degree, had become a kind of currency at a depreciated value, and were negotiated through many hands, previoufly to their return to the treafury. Befides thefe, there were the notes for the ftate and federal debt, which were no inconfiderable fubftitutes for cafh. Many perfons muft have been deluded as to the fcheme for another emiffion of paper money, and it is not uncharitable to fuppofe, that many others were induced to patronize it from principles lefs excufable. A majority of individuals in every community muft, in one fenfe, be benefited, by a depreciating currency.

B 3   It

It puts the publick burden upon principles of chance, and finally fettles it upon the unfortunate adventurers, in whofe hands the bills happen to expire. Hazard, when offered to the human mind, feldom leaves it uninterefted, and from this motive, many will engage on the fide of a paper medium. Creditors indeed, and men of property will be averfe from raifing a phantom, that, in the exchanges of bufinefs, may take place of their real wealth ; and the widow and orphan muft fhudder at the unavoidable fnares of knavifh men, to defraud them of their rights : But thefe claffes of people will ever be oppofed by debtors, fpeculators and perfons otherwife interefted againft them, and unlefs fupported by the juftice and humanity of the people, will be foon overcome. To whatever motives the defire of a paper currency may be attributed, certain it is, that propofitions were very ftrenuoufly made to the legiflature for this purpofe from feveral towns, and upon principles never, perhaps, before advanced. It was requefted that an adequate quantity of this money might be emitted ; and, to avoid the difficulty of redeeming it, that it might by law, be depreciated at fixed rates, in certain given periods, until at a fuitable time, the whole fhould be extinguifhed. So wild a propofal ferved rather to retard than advance the views of the party.

party. A report, however, was once made by a committee of the Houſe of Repreſentatives for emitting a paper currency, but it failed of acceptance. Several other plans were ſuggeſted to the legiſlature from without doors, for relieving the people; but means were at length purſued to bring them forward in a collected and forcible manner by the interference of a new authority. This was no other than the expedient of county conventions.

IN a government as free as the people themſelves can make it, we may expect to find a ſtated and ſatisfactory mode of redreſſing every remediable evil that can happen. In the government of *Maſſachuſetts*, and to what part of the globe are we to advert for a freer one? this mode is pointed out by application to the legiſlature. When publick or private diſtreſs is felt, every town, and every individual in it, have a right to petition the government for redreſs. They have alſo the expreſs privilege of inſtructing their repreſentatives, and of conſequence, directing their meaſures; and, the rules of decency aſide, there is no law to prevent the inhabitants of a townſhip or plantation, adviſing the legiſlature reſpecting the moſt intricate concerns of the nation. The government too, annually reverts into the hands

B 4   of

of thofe who formed it. All publick officers are
thrown back into the clafs of private citizens,
whence they cannot afcend again but by the voice
of the electors : And fo fmall are the qualifica-
tions of voters, that fcarce a fingle man is excluded from his equal fhare in creating even the firft
magiftrate in the community. In a fyftem thus
limited and guarded on all fides, and thus open
to the interference of the citizens even during its
fhort continuance, there feems to be no room for
popular fufpicion. But, in a fociety where that
great prerogative of human nature, felf government, has been literally exercifed, a defire of correcting what appears to be wrong, will naturally
exift. And, if the authority of their own immediate eftablifhment feems averfe from adopting
alterations, there wants that deference to lead the
people to doubt of their projects, which a government eftablifhed by their forefathers, and receiving their implicit obedience from the force of
habit, though lefs perfect in its formation, and
lefs wifely adminiftered, might not fail to infpire.
Such poffibly were the feelings of a number of
towns in the Commonwealth, who reforted to the
mode of affembling by their delegates in convention, for the purpofe of afcertaining their grievances, and the beft manner of redreffing them,

while

while their legiflature were in full poffeffion and exercife of the conftitutional powers, neceffary for the fame purpofe. This practice is faid to be founded on that article in the bill of rights, which provides, " That the people have a right in an orderly and peaceable manner, to affemble to confult upon the common good : Give inftructions to their reprefentatives ; and to requeft of the legiflative body, by the way of addreffes, petitions or remonftrances, redrefs of the wrongs done them, and of the grievances they fuffer." Many, however, have fuppofed, that the fenfe of this article extended only to town meetings which are known to the laws. And indeed, to conftrue it in the moft latitudinary fenfe, might tend in practice, fo to divide the fovereign power of the people, as to make the authority of the laws uncertain, and diftract the attention of fubjects ; efpecially, in a republican government, where all power is actually delegated. But whether conventions of this kind be confiftent with the conftitution or not, certain it is, that their agency has been very material in the late political events. As thofe affemblies received countenance from the perfonal attendance of fome members of the legiflature, who were under oath to fupport the conftitution, it ought not to be readily concluded that their motives were originally injurious to the

eftablifhed

established government; but, it has certainly, been unfortunate to their reputation, that they have been held at such times, and patronized by such characters without doors, as would injure the best institutions. Several disturbances have been ascribed to their influence; one, in particular, which happened in the year 1782, as it bears a strong resemblance to the insurrections that took place in 1786, deserves to be noticed. The well known *Samuel Ely* was indicted at the session of the Supreme Judicial Court at *Northampton* for an attempt to prevent the sitting of the Court of Common Pleas at that place, in which attempt, he used the name of a convention, and pretended to hold up their authority. *Ely* pleaded guilty to this indictment, and while under sentence of Court, when the inhabitants of *Springfield* were accidentally withdrawn from the town, was released from the gaol there, by a mob assembled for the purpose. The ringleaders of this mob being afterwards taken, and confined, an attempt was made to release them also. This obliged the militia of the county to the number of 1200 or 1500 men to march out for the protection of the prison. Both parties met in the field, and nothing but a decided superiority of numbers and characters on the part of government, prevented

bloodshed,

bloodshed, and the commencement of a civil war.
The rioters were surrounded, and then permitted
to repair to their several homes. This event may
not be chargeable upon the convention, as there
is no evidence that *Ely* was authorized by them
to commit the act of violence which he intended;
but, however innocent the intention of members
of convention might have been of these disturbances, if such use was made of their authority, it
was a strong argument against future assemblies of
a like nature.

THE business of the conventions naturally leading them to exhibit lists of grievances to the people, their proceedings of course, always weakened the government, whose business it ever is, to
prevent evils of that kind. But this effect was
greatly increased, when the measures of government itself were held up as grievances. Their
complaints then wore a strong appearance of opposition to constitutional authority. Thus, in the
beginning of the year 1784, we find a proposition
made by the towns of *Wrentham* and *Medway*, to
their sister towns in the county of *Suffolk*, to meet
in convention, to redress the grievance of the commutation to the officers, and of the continental
impost ; measures which had received the sanc-
tion of the legislature, and which no new reasons
could

could be offered to obviate. About the fame
time, *Sutton* made a fimilar propofition to the
towns in the county of *Worcefter*. The anfwer
of the Capital to the circular letter fent to them,
was decidedly againft the propofal. In later times,
the proceedings of conventions have been ftill lefs
juftifiable. We fhall find that they undertook to
cenfure and condemn the conduct of the publick
rulers ; they voted the Senate and the Judicial
Courts to be grievances ; they addreffed the people in language dangerous, even in times of tranquillity ; they called for a revifion of the conftitution, previoufly to the end of its intended duration ; and, under this idea, attempted to collect a
body of men as a general convention, that might
rival the legiflature itfelf. But the proceedings
of thefe affemblies, will particularly appear in the
general account of the infurrections. From the
fhort view which we have taken of the affairs of
the Commonwealth, fufficient caufes appear, to
account for the commotions which enfued. A
heavy debt lying on the ftate, added to burdens
of the fame nature, upon almoft every incorpor-
ation within it ; a decline, or rather an extinction
of publick credit ; a relaxation of manners, and a
free ufe of foreign luxuries ; a decay of trade and
manufactures, with a prevailing fcarcity of money ; and, above all, individuals involved in debt

to

to each other, are evils which leave us under no neceffity of fearching further for the reafons of the infurrections which took place. We ought not to be furprifed to find the people, who but a few years before, upon the abolition of royal government among them, exhibited a moft ftriking example of voluntary fubmiffion to a feeble authority, now driven into a confufion of affairs, common to all countries, but, moft fo perhaps, to thofe who have fhewn the ftrongeft ardour in purfuit of freedom.

THE long reftraints which the confufion of war had laid upon the adminiftration of juftice in private cafes, occafioned a very rapid increafe of civil actions, when thofe reftraints were removed. This circumftance gave employment to the practitioners at the bar, and increafed their numbers beyond what had been ufual in the ftate. The profeffion naturally became a fubject of obfervation; and, at length, was generally fpoken of as an object of reform. Advantage was taken of the prevailing jealoufy againft lawyers; and unfortunately, a prelude to the infurrections was framed out of it. Inflammatory writings were inferted in the newfpapers, to excite an idea, in the minds of the people, that the burdens which they laboured under, were occafioned by the abufes of

this

this profeſſion : And, a doctrine was particularly inſiſted on in one of them, that this claſs of men ought to be aboliſhed. The electors were therefore conjured to leave them out of publick office, and to inſtruct their repreſentatives, then about to be choſen for the year 1786, to annihilate them. This idea communicated itſelf from very natural cauſes. The lawyers were odious to debtors as the legal inſtruments of their diſtreſſes. They were alſo intimately connected with the courts of juſtice, and, in a great meaſure, under their control : A clamour againſt the one, therefore, was a kind of impeachment of the other. The tranſition from the ſervants of the courts, to the courts themſelves, being eaſy and direct, the cry, of courſe, was received and ſpread with avidity, by thoſe whoſe intentions were directed at the adminiſtration of juſtice in general. The flame pervaded the greateſt part of the Commonwealth. The lawyers, in moſt inſtances, were excluded from the Houſe of Repreſentatives. Among other towns, the capital filled the ſeat which ſhe had from ancient times, reſerved for one of this profeſſion, the ſeat where *Pratt, Thacher, Otis* and *Adams*, had drawn admiration and love from the publick eye, with a gentleman of a leſs unpopular calling. When the aſſembly

met,

met, their zeal was kindled from the people.
This was firft evidenced by their elections in filling up the vacancies in Senate. Preference was
given to fome characters, which could not be accounted for on any other grounds, than that of
their fellow candidates being practitioners of the
law. As foon as bufinefs came forward, an emulation was fhewn to be foremoft in correcting a-
bufes which occupied fo large a fhare of the publick attention. Various inftances were adduced,
wherein the principles of the fee bill, from the local circumftances of the parties, operated to diftrefs them ; and much was faid to convince the
Houfe, that thefe diftreffes had been greatly en-
creafed, by the exorbitant fees of attornies. After many warm altercations upon this fubject, the
Houfe, with a view of reducing the exactions and
influence of the regular practitioners, at length
paffed a bill to admit all perfons of a moral character into the practice of the law, before the Judicial Courts ; to fix the fees of attornies ; to provide for their taking an oath previoufly to their
pleading, in every caufe, that they would not receive more than lawful fees of their employers ;
and to reftrain the practice of champarty. But,
when this bill was fent up, the Senate, defirous
of a further confideration of the fubject, took
meafures

measures for examining it in the recess, and referred their decision to their next assembling.

THE other proceedings of either house, were hardly so correspondent with the views of the discontented party. The session was made memorable by the grant of the supplementary funds to the *United States*; a measure, which, though dictated by the principles of national credit, did not fail to stand high in the catalogue of future grievances. The advocates for a paper money system also lost their confidence in the House. A petition was presented from delegates of all the towns in the county of *Bristol*, praying for an emission of that kind of currency. This measure was probably suggested by the example of their neighbours in the state of *Rhodeisland*, who had just emitted a large quantity; and it was expected, no doubt, that this precedent would have influenced the legislature to favour the proposal; but, on a trial of parties in the House, there were found to be, out of one hundred and eighteen members, only nineteen advocates for the scheme, and only thirty five, out of one hundred and twenty four, in support of the still more popular plan of making real and personal estate a tender, at an appraisement, in discharge of executions. Indeed,

the

the fate of thefe projects feems to have been fingularly perverfe at this feffion ; for, they were not only negatived, but a law was paffed enabling the citizens to difcharge executions in favour of any inhabitants of fuch ftates as had iffued paper money or made a tender act, by payment in their own currency, or a tender of eftate according to the regulations which they themfelves had provided. This fyftem of retaliation at once vindicated the rights of the people, and expreffed the difapprobation of the legiflature, at eftablifhing engines of fraud upon publick faith and authority. An attempt alfo failed to divert the appropriation of the impoft and excife duties, from the payment of the intereft of the confolidated notes, for the purpofe of difcharging the foreign demands, and thofe of the civil lift. In this fituation, the legiflature adjourned, on the 8th of *July,* to the 31ft of *January* following.

THE lofs of fo many motions refpecting the important concerns of the Commonwealth, could not but have a proportionable effect upon thofe members whofe confidence in the rejected plans, had drawn them to their defence. The grant of the fupplementary funds was alfo a kind of triumph over this fide of the Houfe. A divifion, of courfe, took place among the members of the leg-

C   iflature,

iflature, which muft, even upon the moft favourable view of human nature, have accelerated the divifions among the people at large. The failure of the minority was in a great meafure owing to the determined conduct of the Senate, who foon began to be a diftinguifhed fubject of clamour. The outcry againft lawyers was at length drowned in more general complaints, and grievances arofe on all quarters, from a variety of caufes.

ON the 22d of *Auguft*, a convention of delegates from fifty towns in the county of *Hampfhire*, met at *Hatfield*, and came to the following decifions.

" AT a meeting of delegates from fifty towns in the county of *Hampfhire*, in convention held at *Hatfield*, in faid county, on Tuefday the 22d day of *Auguft* inftant, and continued by adjournments until the twenty fifth, &c. Voted, that this meeting is conftitutional.

" THE convention from a thorough conviction of great uneafinefs, fubfifting among the people of this county and Commonwealth, then went into an inquiry for the caufe ; and, upon mature confideration, deliberation and debate, were of opinion, that many grievances and unneceffary burdens now lying upon the people, are the fources of that difcontent fo evidently difcoverable throughout

out this Commonwealth. Among which the following articles were voted as ſuch, viz.

1ſt. The exiſtence of the Senate.

2d. The preſent mode of repreſentation.

3d. The officers of government not being annually dependent on the repreſentatives of the people, in General Court aſſembled, for their ſalaries.

4th. All the civil officers of government, not being annually elected by the Repreſentatives of the people, in General Court aſſembled.

5th. The exiſtence of the Courts of Common Pleas, and General Seſſions of the Peace.

6th. The Fee Table as it now ſtands.

7th. The preſent mode of appropriating the impoſt and exciſe.

8th. The unreaſonable grants made to ſome of the officers of government.

9th. The ſupplementary aid.

10th. The preſent mode of paying the governmental ſecurities.

11th. The preſent mode adopted for the payment and ſpeedy collection of the laſt tax.

12th. The preſent mode of taxation as it operates unequally between the polls and eſtates, and between landed and mercantile intereſts.

13th. The preſent method of practice of the attornies at law.

C 2

14th.

14th. The want of a sufficient medium of trade, to remedy the mischiefs arising from the scarcity of money.

15th. The General Court sitting in the town of *Boston*.

16th. The present embarraffments on the prefs.

17th. The neglect of the settlement of important matters depending between the Commonwealth and Congrefs, relating to monies and averages.

18th. Voted, This convention recommend to the several towns in this county, that they instruct their Reprefentatives, to ufe their influence in the next General Court, to have emitted a bank of paper money, fubject to a depreciation ; making it a tender in all payments, equal to filver and gold, to be iffued in order to call in the Commonwealth's fecurities.

19th. Voted, That whereas feveral of the above articles of grievances, arife from defects in the conftitution ; therefore a revifion of the fame ought to take place.

20th. Voted, That it be recommended by this convention to the feveral towns in this county, that they petition the Governour to call the General Court immediately together, in order that the

other

other grievances complained of, may by the legislature, be redreffed.

21ft. Voted, That this convention recommend it to the inhabitants of this county, that they abftain from all mobs and unlawful affemblies, until a conftitutional method of redrefs can be obtained.

22d. Voted, That Mr. *Caleb Weft* be defired to tranfmit a copy of the proceedings of this convention to the convention of the county of *Worcefter*.

23d. Voted, That the chairman of this convention be defired to tranfmit a copy of the proceedings of this convention to the county of *Berkfhire*.

24th. Voted, That the chairman of this convention be directed to notify a county convention, upon any motion made to him for that purpofe, if he judge the reafons offered be fufficient, giving fuch notice, together with the reafons therefor, in the publick papers of this county.

25th. Voted, That a copy of the proceedings of this convention be fent to the prefs in *Springfield* for publication."

ALTHOUGH it is hinted in the foregoing proceedings, that they do not contain all the caufes of grievance, yet they may be fo far confidered as a faithful collection of thefe caufes, that injuftice

will

will not be done to the fubject, if fome of the future proceedings of that nature fhould not be inferted at large. Thefe can require but little com-
ment. It is fcarcely poffible for a government to
be more imperfect, or worfe adminiftered, than
that of *Maffachufetts* is here reprefented to be.
Effential branches of the legiflative and judicial
departments were faid to be grievous ; material
proceedings upon national concerns erroneous ;
obvious meafures for paying the debt blindly
overlooked ; publick monies mifappropriated, and
the conftitution itfelf intolerably defective. The
directions for tranfmitting thefe proceedings to
the convention of *Worcefter*, and to the county of
Berkfhire, difplayed a defign in this affembly, of
doing more than paffively reprefenting their own
grievances.

AFTER this cenfure of a convention of delegates
from fifty towns, upon the Courts of Common
Pleas and General Seffions of the Peace, agreed
upon in three days time, and juft before their
ftated terms, it was not furprifing, notwithftanding the caution of the convention againft mobs,
to find that reverence which, if nothing elfe could,
the antiquity and paft utility of thofe courts ought
to have infpired, at once fuperfeded by popular
rage and contempt. Accordingly, on the laft

Tuefday

Tuefday of Auguft, a competent number of infurgents, fuppofed to be near 1500, affembled under arms at *Northampton*; took poffeffion of the
Court Houfe, and effectually prevented the fitting
of the courts aforementioned at that place, as pre-
fcribed by law. Upon this violence being committed, a proclamation was iffued by his Excellency the Governour, calling in the moft feeling
and fpirited manner, upon the officers and citizens of the Commonwealth, to fupprefs fuch treafonable proceedings. But, little attention was
given by the ill difpofed to this timely meafure.
The counties of *Worcefter, Middlefex, Briftol* and
Berkfhire were fet in a flame, and the tumult
threatened to be general.

on the fucceeding week, the Courts of Common Pleas and General Seffions of the Peace, being by law to be holden at *Worcefter*, a body of
infurgents to the number of 300 and upwards,
pofted themfelves at the Court Houfe in that
place. The judges were admitted to the door,
'where a line of bayonets prevented their entrance.
The chief juftice remonftrated with the rioters,
on the madnefs of their conduct; but the court
were obliged to retire to an adjacent houfe, where
they opened agreeably to law, and adjourned to
the next morning. The violence of the mob,

however, foon obliged the Court of Common
Pleas to adjourn without day, and the Court of
Seffions to adjourn to the 21ft of *November* fol-
lowing.

THE nature of thefe difturbances rendered their
remedy peculiarly difficult. The oppofition to
the courts muft have been unjuftifiable even in
the views of the infurgents themfelves. But,
this was a general caufe, in which every man exercifed his right of judging, and there were not
wanting plaufible reafons to induce the lefs informed to judge wrong. The ftopping of the
Judicial Courts had been blended, in the minds
of fome people, with the redrefs of grievances ;
and had been charitably, but incautioufly confidered, only as a mode of awakening the attention
of the legiflature to that object. Under fuch
pretexts, many moderate men, and more from lefs
pardonable principles than that of moderation,
excufed themfelves from military duty. This en-
ervated the operations of the militia ; and, joined
to the circumftance of their being in fome inftances, unorganized, had almoft deprived the Commonwealth of any advantage from this palladium
of republican freedom. The attack in the county of *Hampfhire* was fo fudden and violent, that,
from this caufe perhaps, no recurrence was had

to

to the militia ; but, in *Worcester*, it was maturely concluded, that those in that vicinity, could not then be relied on. This in a manner, disarmed the Supreme Executive Magistrate, who from inclination, and the principles of the constitution, directed himself to the militia for assistance. The effects of this evil were afterwards still more conspicuous. When bodies of the militia were marched by order of their proper officers, numbers whose principles were concealed, would, at some critical juncture, openly change their sides in the field ; a treacherous practice, that was checked by a subsequent provision in the law martial.

THE contagion of this riotous disposition appearing to spread, notwithstanding the militia had been ordered to the aid of the Sheriffs, the Governour turned his attention to suitable means of checking its nearer approach to the capital. Accordingly an advising body was collected, in the absence of the council, consisting of such counsellors as were in town, the Judges of the Supreme Judicial Court ; the Attorney General and other publick characters. The Courts of Common Pleas and General Sessions of the Peace, were then next to be holden at *Concord* and *Taunton* on the same day. There could be no doubt, that

attempts

attempts would be made to impede their fitting. Among other events which had taken place in *Middlesex*, a convention confisting of the delegates of a majority of the towns in that county, had set the day after that which was held at *Hatfield*. Their proceedings bore a very near refemblance to thofe of their brethren in *Hampshire*. The Senate were not numbered among their grievances, but the Court of Common Pleas was exprefsly mentioned. The people of *Middlefex* however, were fuppofed to be lefs averfe from the adminiftering of juftice than thofe of the upper counties; and not oppofed to fupporting the Judicial Courts againft a force. This fuppofition was founded on good information, obtained by early and judicious inquiries, made by the Major General of that divifion, who appeared before the council on the occafion. It was alfo thought that the local circumftances of *Concord* made it an eligible fpot for the ferious exertion of government. In purfuance of this idea, it was agreed, that the militia fhould be called out in defence of the courts from fuch parts, and in fuch numbers, as would beft ferve to protect them. But, while this plan was executing, an agreement was entered into by the inhabitants of *Concord* and feveral towns in their neighbourhood, to meet by their committees,

committees, to confer with any perfons who might appear in arms, with a view of perfuading them into moderate meafures. Much was hoped for by the acting council from a pacifick negotiation ; and, upon the perfonal reprefentation of two juftices of the Common Pleas, the orders for calling out the militia, who were defigned to act in *Middlefex*, were abfolutely countermanded, and thofe iffued for *Briftol* conditionally fo. No fooner was it known by the infurgents, who were contemptible in point of ftrength and character, that government would not act with force, than they appeared in triumph on the fpot. Thofe of the county were reinforced by a fmall party from *Worcefter*. They took poffeffion of the Court Houfe, and paraded with great infolence before the court who had affembled at a fmall diftance. One of their leaders was exceedingly outrageous, and once threatened to put all perfons to the fword who fhould not join them in two hours. Such was the profanity of his language, that it at firft ftaggered the lefs hardened party from *Worcefter*, but a union of forces afterwards took place. *Job Shattuck*, their principal leader, fent a written meffage, that it was the fenfe of the people, that the courts fhould not fit. He afterwards affected to permit the Court of Seffions to fit, on condi-

tion

tion of adjourning to a day prescribed ; but, the issue was, that the rioters grew still more outrageous, and no court could sit at all.

IN the county of *Bristol*, the cause of government did not yield so easily. Notwithstanding the counter orders respecting the turning out of the militia, the spirit of the people in some parts, led them to appear in arms under the direction of Major General *David Cobb*, to the number of three hundred, and the insurgents, though a third part more, could not prevent the sitting of the courts. These, however, voluntarily adjourned again without day.

WHILE these insurrections were happening in the lower counties, the rage of the malcontents was not less violent in the county of *Berkshire*. A convention was held at *Lenox*, on the last week in *August*. This assembly however, was composed of members, as well from the towns where the friends to government prevailed, as from the disaffected ; and their proceedings seem to have evidenced a different disposition, from that of the other conventions. Although the general rage for reformation was conspicuous, yet they explicitly approved of the appropriation of the revenue arising from the impost and excise duties, and of the grant of the supplementary

funds

funds to the *United States* ; and they manifefted a decent and refpe&ful regard towards
the adminiftration of government in general.
They difapproved of the fyftems for eftablifhing
paper money and tender a&ts. They. folemnly
engaged to ufe their influence to fupport the courts
of juftice, in the exercife of their legal powers, and
to endeavour to quiet the agitated fpirits of the
people. The infurgents, however, affembled in
force to the number of eight hundred, at *Great
Barrington*, and not only prevented the fitting of
the courts which were fo obnoxious to them, but
broke open the gaol, and liberated the prifoners.
They alfo compelled three of the Judges of the
Court of Common Pleas, to fign an obligation,
that they would not a&t under their commiffions,
until grievances were redreffed. It ought, however, in juftice to the infurgents, to be mentioned,
that the fourth Judge, who was a member of the
Senate, upon a proper refiftance, was not forced
to fign the obligation. This circumftance muft
extenuate the crime, in the opinion of the world,
as it will abate the degree of compulfion, which
otherwife might be fuppofed to have been ufed
upon this occafion.

THE condu&t of the inhabitants of the town of
Bofton, during thefe difturbances, fhould not pafs
unnoticed.

unnoticed. They addressed the Governour, and in the most unequivocal manner, declared their determination to cooperate in support of constitutional government; whilst they also declared, that their feelings led them to hope for lenient measures to be adopted, with respect to their deluded friends and fellow citizens. They also sent a circular letter addressed to the inhabitants of every town, wherein they acknowledged their own obligations, and recited the mutual danger that awaited all parties, during the war. They contrasted the present free state of the citizens, with what it would have been, had they become a conquered people. They held up the sacred pledges of life and fortune, made to support a constitution, which was as inestimable as the blood that had purchased it. And they conjured their brethren not to gratify the malice of their common enemies, in seeking a redress of supposed grievances, by other means than those which their social compact had amply provided. To their address, his Excellency returned a very favourable answer, in which, however, he plainly suggested, that the supineness of those citizens, who had been duly called upon to assist the Sheriffs, and had neglected to do it, drew on them the blame of the unhappy consequences. The letter to the several towns

produced

produced various replies, but moſt of them con‑ veyed a union of ſentiment, and a tender of aid to ſupport the conſtitution.

THE diſpoſition for inſurrections at this time, was not confined to *Maſſachuſetts*. On the 20th of *September*, about four hundred men, armed in different modes, ſurrounded the legiſlature of *Newhampſhire*, for ſeveral hours, with a view of forcing them into a paper money ſyſtem, agreea‑ bly to a petition which had been previouſly pre‑ ferred by a convention of delegates from about thirty towns, in that ſtate. But the ſpirit of their citizens immediately led them to appear in arms, and cruſhed the inſurrection in its infancy.

SO frequent an oppoſition to the adminiſtering of juſtice, made it neceſſary that an immediate ſeſſion of the General Court ſhould be held. The Governour, in conſequence of a requiſition of Congreſs for a tax, had iſſued his proclamation for calling that court together on the 18th of *Oc‑ tober*, but the tumults afterwards induced him to fix upon the 27th of *September* for their aſſem‑ bling.

WHILE the legiſlature were convening, the in‑ ſurgents were extending their object. Hitherto their grievances had been confined to the Courts

of

of Common Pleas, the Courts of General Seſſions of the Peace, and to ſome ſuppoſed inconvenien- cies in the mode of holding the Courts of Probate. But, their oppoſition to the two firſt of theſe, had, as they pretended, made a further meaſure necef- ſary to their ſafety. This was to prevent the ſit- ting of the Supreme Judicial Court itſelf, and thereby ſhield themſelves from any indictment on account of their paſt offences, in obſtructing the adminiſtration of juſtice. No great danger ought to have been apprehended by them from this quarter, as the court laſt mentioned had ſet at *Worceſter* without the jury's finding a ſingle bill againſt them. However, it was determined by the inſurgents, to prevent their doing buſineſs at *Springfield*, if poſſible; and the Governour, on the other hand, took meaſures to obviate their deſigns. Accordingly he ordered the Court Houſe to be taken into poſſeſſion by 600 men, under the command of Major General *William Shepard*. This party were well officered and e- quipped, and contained the moſt reſpectable char- acters for abilities and intereſt, in the county of *Hampſhire*. On the day of the court's ſitting, the inſurgents alſo appeared, equal if not ſuperiour in numbers, but vaſtly inferiour in officers and arms. They were headed by one *Daniel Shays*, who had

been

been a Captain in the late continental army; but had refigned his commiffion for reafons quite problematical. They were highly incenfed at government's taking poffeffion of the Court Houfe previoufly to their arrival. They fent a requeft to the Judges, that none of the late rioters fhould be indiƈted ; but received a very firm reply, purporting that the Judges fhould execute the laws of the country agreeably to their oaths. In the confufion, however, neceffarily attending two fuch large bodies of armed men, who, before they retired increafed to more than 2000, the court could tranfaƈt but little bufinefs. On Wednefday the panel of Jurors not being filled, thofe jurymen who appeared were difmiffed. On the next day, which was the third of their fitting, the court adjourned, after refolving that it was not expedient to proceed to the county of *Berkfhire*. The mortification which the infurgents fuffered from the Court Houfe being preoccupied by the militia, led them to feveral bold meafures. At one time, they marched down upon the militia with loaded mufquets, and every preparation was made for an engagement; but they were diffuaded from an attack, as it was faid, at the inftance of their commander. They infifted upon paffing through the ftreet of *Springfield*, in face of General *Shepard's* troops, and were allowed fo to do, on condition

D   of

of their behaving peaceably, which was observed.
After the rising of the Court, they also demanded
the ground on which the General was posted.
As it was necessary for him to change his position
in order to secure the federal arsenal, for which
people were very apprehensive, he marched to
the protection of that, and the insurgents succeeded his forces in the occupation of a place
which had, in fact, become of no real importance.
The condition of the town of *Springfield* was
truly melancholy, during this civil contention.
Neighbours were opposed to each other under
arms, the houses were rendered the scenes of fe-
male distress; and it was in the power of accident
only, to have brought on an action, which might
have destroyed the lives of thousands, and sub-
jected all property to the immediate vengeance
of the party, that might have become victorious.
After remaining in this situation for four days,
the inhabitants were relieved by the dispersing
of both parties.

AT the time appointed by law for holding the
Supreme Judicial Court, at *Greatbarrington*, the
malcontents, affecting to believe, that the court
intended to deceive them, and that business would
be transacted as usual, notwithstanding the resolution to the contrary, assembled in considerable
numbers;

numbers; and being difappointed in their object, became extremely riotous. Several perfons who were obnoxious to their views, were obliged to fly, and one gentleman who fuftained a very honourable office, was purfued in various directions, by armed men. Houfes were fearched, and, in fome inftances citizens were fired upon.

WHEN the legiflature had affembled, the Governour opened to them the whole tranfactions that had then taken place, in a fpeech from the chair. In this he ftated the danger of fuch proceedings, and the want of juftification on the part of the infurgents, even upon the fuppofition that grievances exifted, as they had complained. He related the meafures which he had taken, and obferved, that if the people would not be obedient to orders iffued for their own fafety, the confequences were imputable only to themfelves. The Senate appeared to be decided in their opinion, of the meafures which were neceffary to be taken, refpecting the infurgents; but parties did not ftand fo unequally balanced on this point, in the lower Houfe. Thofe members who from time to time, had found their plans overruled there, feemed to think that publick affairs had not been fo properly conducted as they might have been; and to hope, that the prefent commotions might be the

means

means of bringing about what, they always thought, should have been effected without them. They were, therefore, cautious in their proceedings against the insurgents, and, probably did not wish them to be crushed, till things were corrected, according to *their* view of a right system.

THE first measures which the Senate adopted, were, to agree to a report of a joint committee on the Governour's speech. This report was expressive of the abhorrence which the two Houses entertained, of the proceedings against the Judicial Courts. It decidedly approved of his Excellency's conduct, in raising the militia for their defence. A promise of pay was also made to those who had been, or should afterwards be called into service. It recommended a revisal of the militia law, and expressed a full determination on the part of the legislature, to examine into, and redress all grievances, which might lie upon the people : And it provided that the privilege of the writ of *Habeas corpus*, should be suspended for a limited time. The House were unanimous in agreeing to the first mentioned clause in this report ; the other clauses were also voted, excepting the last, at which a determined stand was made. In vain was it urged, that the daring attempts which had been made upon the authority

of

of government, required a decisive defence on
their part ; that the measures proposed, were only means of disarming, without punishing the
leaders of the insurgents ; that the same means
had been adopted in less perilous times, under the
present constitution, without hesitation ; and that
the safety of the friends of government, in the
discontented counties, made them again necessary. There were other gentlemen, and they were
then the majority, who thought it a very unsuita-
ble time for coercive measures. The first object,
in their opinions, ought to be, to remove all causes
of discontent, and so leave the insurgents without an appearance of justification, in case of their
perseverance. But, if violent plans should be
projected, they feared that the uneasiness would
increase, and the great body of neuters would be
disgusted with the government, and lost to its
cause. After long debates this part of the report
was again committed.

THE party who were for postponing vigorous
measures against the insurgents, having given this
check to their opponents, it became an object to
hasten forward whatever business was considered
as a condition of the suspension of the writ of *Habeas corpus*. The grievances of the *People*, as the
discontented were fond of calling themselves, had

been

been laid before the court in several modes. Petitions from sundry towns had stated them, and
these were committed by both houses. The conventions also appeared upon this occasion. Eighteen towns in *Middlesex*, forty one towns in *Worcester*, and all the towns but one in *Bristol*, formed conventions in their respective counties, by
their delegates. A petition from each was preferred for a redress of grievances, which were stated
as nearly alike, by all, as circumstances would
permit. That from *Bristol* was peculiarly guarded at this point. They united in the gross, with
the petition from *Worcester*, and then observed,
that in case there should be different petitions
from different counties, or perplexity in the subject matter of those petitions, or they should appear insufficiently explicit, they further prayed
the court, to call a convention of the Commonwealth, for the purpose of uniting in consistent
and explicit petitions, for the removal of those
grievances which the people laboured under. The
petition from *Worcester*, after reciting their grievances, prayed that the sense of all the towns in the
Commonwealth might be taken, respecting the necessity of revising the constitution ; and, in case two
thirds of them should be in favour of a revision, that
a state convention might be called for revising it.

They

They received a delegate from the county of *Bristol,* and chofe a committee to correfpond with
other counties—a meafure that was eminently in-
ftrumental in fubverting the Britifh government
in this country. They alfo undertook to aid the
legiflature in the well ordering of the Commonwealth, by addreffing the people of their county,
and expreffing their confidence, that they would
peaceably wait the refult of that feffion of the
General Court.

As the fubftance of the petitions from the conventions was included in thofe from the towns, it
faved a difficulty that might otherwife have arif-
en, as to the conftitutionality of thofe bodies, and
their authority to petition in behalf of the places
they were faid to reprefent ; efpecially, as in fome
inftances, their conftituents had not empowered
them to go further than to agree upon a petition,
fubject to their own revifal, and to be prefented
from the refpective towns themfelves. Thefe petitions therefore were fuffered to lie, without any
decifion upon them.

The grievances which were finally fingled out
for the confideration of the court, as being the
moft important, and moftly within their power
to remedy were, the fitting of the General Court

in

in the town of *Boston* ; the inftitution and regulation of the Courts of Common Pleas and General Seffions of the Peace, with the mode of holding the Probate Courts ; the burdens of the people arifing from the fcarcity of money, and the difficulties thereby accruing in the payment of back taxes, and private debts ; the mode of appropriating the proceeds of the impoft and excife duties ; the fee bill, and the falaries of the officers of government.

As one principal caufe of the difturbances among the people, was the mifreprefentations of defigning men, by which they had been led to believe the groffeft falfehoods, it was agreed on all hands, that an addrefs fhould alfo be fent to all the citizens, for their information, relative to publick affairs.

Among the falaries of publick officers, that of the firft magiftrate, which was eftablifhed at 1100l. per annum, being objected to by many difcontented perfons, it was early taken into confideration by the Houfe of Reprefentatives. They made it a queftion, whether it was within the power of the legiflature to reduce it, confiftently with the 13th article of the firft fection and 2d chapter of the conftitution. After a full difcuf-

fion

fion of this point, it was determined that the falary might be reduced, notwithstanding it had been
fixed by an act in pursuance of the constitution.
But, no use was made of this vote at the present
time, and it was declared by members who were
in the affirmative, that it was intended to extend
to a future year only, and not to any service
which was actually commenced. Care was tak-
en in the subsequent address to the people, to state
the reasonableness of the salary in itself, and particularly when compared to that allowed by the
late province, which was not only larger but attended with a variety of perquisites.

THE opposers of a paper money system and a
tender act, finding both those measures strongly
urged by almost all the petitions upon publick
grievances, and that the insurgents were not rig-
orously treated, began to think of a compromise,
by allowing of the latter plan, in order to avoid a
still more odious expedient, in the former. The
committee who had been appointed on the subject, submitted a question, Whether a tender act,
or an act for the suspension of law, would not be
inconsistent with the constitution ; and also mili-
tate with the confederation and treaty of peace,
unless the debts due to British creditors before the
war, should be excepted ? The Senate voted, that
it

it would be againſt the confederation and treaty, unleſs the exception ſhould be made. But the Houſe felt no ways diſpoſed to give a preference, in this caſe, to Britiſh ſubjects over their own citizens, and diſagreed with the Senate, at the ſame time giving leave for a draught of ſuch a bill to be laid on their table.

WHILE the Houſe of Repreſentatives were preparing this bill, and endeavouring to reform or aboliſh the Courts of Common Pleas and General Seſſions of the Peace, the time arrived for the Supreme Judicial Court to ſit at *Taunton.* On this occaſion the Senate propoſed a meſſage to the Governour to requeſt that his Excellency would give his moſt ſerious attention to the ſupport of their ſeſſion, and the Houſe concurred in this propoſal. The Governour, of courſe, afterwards communicated the meaſures which he had taken. The Senate, in return, originated a meſſage of thanks, in which they introduced, with ſome addreſs, the reſolves that had paſſed in both Houſes, but which, from their connexion with the vote for ſuſpending the writ of *Habeas corpus,* ſtill remained on the Repreſentative's table, incapable of being laid before the chair. This meſſage proved eventually, of great conſequence, as it was the foundation of very ſpirited meaſures on the part

of

of the Governour. In it the two houfes declared, that they would always on fuch and other occafions, afford the Supreme Executive all that aid, which fhould be incumbent on them, in their own department; fully confiding that his Excellency would ftill perfevere in the exercife of fuch powers, as were vefted in him by their excellent conftitution, for enforcing due obedience to the authority and laws of government, &c. In addition to this meffage, the Court paffed a riot act, which was the firft coercive meafure they took, for counteracting the tumults of the infurgents.

THE Supreme Judicial Court were effectually fupported at *Taunton*, the infurgents appearing at a diftance only. One of them was permitted to prefent a petition to the court, in which it was requefted, as the fenfe of the people, that their fitting fhould be adjourned. But, the memorialift being afked, How it happened, that the jurors had all attended, if it was the defire of the people that the court fhould not fit? he was confounded, and retired.

SUCH preparations were made for meeting the infurgents at *Cambridge*, the week enfuing, that they dared not attempt to impede the fitting of the Supreme Judicial Court at that place. The

Governour

Governour took the opportunity of reviewing the troops that marched upon this occasion, under the command of Major General *John Brooks*. They amounted to 2069, besides volunteers. The respectable appearance of this body, which was made up of the *Middlesex* militia, and three companies from *Boston*, with many pieces of Artillery, greatly elevated the spirits of all the friends of the government, and irritated or depressed those who were opposed to it.

WHILE the Supreme Executive was employed in making the necessary military arrangements, for supporting the administration of justice, the House of Representatives remained in the same pacifick disposition towards the insurgents. Nothing of consequence was suffered to pass them, but what was connected with the grievances of the people. They completed an act providing for the payment of the back taxes in specifick articles, at fixed rates, on account of the scarcity of money. They agreed upon a plan for originating civil causes before Justices of the Peace, in order to lessen the business of the Courts of Common Pleas, and to render law processes less expensive. And they industriously employed themselves in framing a tender act, that should be the least exceptionable to the various opposers of that measure.

meafure. All of thefe acts finally paffed the legiflature, though feveral cafes were excepted from
the tender law, and the operation of it was limited
to eight months at the motion of the Senate.

ON the 28th of *October*, the Governour communicated to the Court a Refolve of Congrefs,
for increafing the federal troops already raifed, for
carrying on an Indian war, to 2040 ; of the additional number, the proportion required of *Maffachufetts*, was 660. The critical juncture at which
this requifition was made, and the large quota of
men affigned to the Commonwealth, excited
the jealoufy of many perfons, that the forces
were to be employed in fuppreffing domeftick
difficulties, previoufly to their marching to the
frontiers ; and this fufpicion gained fome ground
among the members. The refolve, however,
was fully complied with.

IN purfuance of the idea of quieting the uneafinefs of the people, the Houfe of Reprefentatives
went on to vote, that they would remove the
General Court out of the town of *Bofton*, if it could
be done with advantage to the publick ; and appointed a committee, confifting of a member from
each county, to report a more fuitable place at their
next fitting. They alfo took up much time in
debating

debating upon the beft mode of appropriating the proceeds of the impoft and excife duties ; one party contending in favour of the old one, and others aiming to defray, with thofe duties, the intereft of the foreign loans, and the exigencies of government.

SUCH delays taking place in the effecting of a vigorous fyftem for fupporting the authority of the laws, occafioned very great alarms among thofe who were moft oppofed to the infurrections. Many were furprifed that fuch daring violations of the laws, as had taken place, were not followed with the moft decifive punifhment; or, at leaft, that fome forcible meafures were not purfued to prevent them in future. They were uneafy that an intereft could be found, ftrong enough to confine the vote for fufpending the privilege of the writ of *Habeas Corpus*, to the Reprefentatives table. They began to lofe confidence in the General Court, and to wifh that means might be found to adjourn them, before the publick caufe fhould be injured by a feeble fyftem, which might tend only to hold up their divifions and want of energy.

THERE began alfo to arife another clafs of men, in the community, who gave very ferious apprehenfions

henfions to the advocates for a republican form of government. Thefe though few in number, and but the feeds of a party, confifted of perfons refpectable for their literature and their wealth. They had feen fo much confufion arifing from popular councils, and had been fo long expecting meafures, for vindicating the dignity of government, which feemed now lefs likely to take place than ever, that they, with an impatience too inconfiderately indulged, were almoft ready to affent to a revolution, in hopes of erecting a political fyftem, more braced than the prefent, and better calculated, in their opinions, to promote the peace and happinefs of the citizens.

BUT the infurgents themfelves at length brought about, what their oppofers, perhaps, could not have effected without them. The debates in the Houfe of Representatives refpecting the fufpenfion of the privilege of the writ of *Habeas Corpus*, had been fpread abroad with the moft aggravating circumftances. The infurgents, either through fear for their perfonal fecurity, which was the oftenfible object, or for the purpofe of ripening the oppofition to government, fpread the alarm with avidity. A circular letter was fent by their party, to the felectmen of many towns in the county of *Hampfhire*, requiring them immediately

diately to affemble their inhabitants, to fee that they were furnifhed with arms and ammunition according to law. They alfo ordered the militia, in fome inftances, to be furnifhed with fixty rounds of powder, and to ftand ready to march at a moment's warning. In addition to this, another convention was alfo appointed to be held at *Hadley.*

INFORMATION of thefe circumftances was given to the Court, by the Governour, on the 7th of *November,* and the committee to whom his Excellency's meffage was referred, recommended that the report formerly made upon his fpeech, and which then lay before the Houfe, fhould be taken up. This report by the recommitment which we have mentioned, now contained, among other articles, a claufe for trying perfons charged with obftructing the adminiftration of juftice, out of the county where the fact was committed, and a claufe for obliging all perfons concerned in the infurrections, to take the oath of allegiance, as a condition of being indemnified againft legal profecutions.

IN the debates upon this report, at the prefent time, a great ftruggle took place. The advocates for lenient meafures could hardly yet be

brought

brought to think, that the crifis had arrived, when it was neceffary, that the perfonal rights of the fubject, fhould be fo far deferted by the laws, as to allow of trials in foreign counties ; or that every man's liberty fhould be trufted to the difcretion of the Supreme Executive, without legal remedy. At length however, the extreme danger to which the government was reduced, by thefe hardy and infulting meafures of the infurgents, outweighed every confideration that had hitherto fupported an oppofition to the fpirit of the report. The claufe was agreed to, which empowered the Supreme Judicial Court to try perfons in any county within the Commonwealth, who had been guilty of obftructing or impeding, or attempting to obftruct or impede, the adminiftration of law and juftice ; or of attempting the detriment or annoyance of the Commonwealth, by open violence or private confpiracy. Though, when the bill was brought in, it was provided that the trial fhould be had in the county neareft to that in which the fact was committed, where there fhould be no apprehenfion of danger. In conformity to that part of the report which recommended a fufpenfion of the privilege of the writ of *Habeas corpus*, another bill was framed, and finally paffed into a law, which empowered the Governour and Council, to imprifon without

E   bail

bail or mainprife, any perfons whom they fhould deem the fafety of the Commonwealth required to be reftrained of their perfonal liberty, or whofe enlargement was dangerous thereto. The duration of this law was limited to the firft day of *July* following.

BUT thefe meafures were not adopted without a qualification which might prevent their operating to the detriment of any individual in the community. A bill was at the fame time brought in for granting a pardon to all perfons concerned in the late difturbances, who fhould by the firft day of *January* following take the oath of allegiance, and be of good behaviour in the mean time. The conditions of this general act of indemnity, were mild and eafy to be complied with, and the advocates for it were exceedingly fanguine as to its effects. They thought the infurrections arofe from mifapprehenfions and ignorance of the evil confequences of violent meafures ; and they had too favourable an idea of their countrymen, to fuppofe that they would not retract, when they were undeceived, and when fo fair a way was opened for their return to their duty and allegiance.

IN order to give time for information, and for the heated fpirits of the malcontents to fubfide, the

the Courts of Common Pleas and General Seffions of the Peace, were for the prefent, in a manner, put out of their way. Thofe in the county of *Hampſhire*, were adjourned to the 26th of *December*; thofe in *Berkſhire*, to the firſt Tuefday in *February*; thofe in *Plymouth* and *Briſtol* were alfo adjourned, though for a ſhorter time. This arrangement brought the firſt ſtated term of thefe courts at *Cambridge*, a place which from its neighbourhood to the feat of government, and the difpofition of its inhabitants, was fuppofed to be a favourable fpot for the introduction of good order. The Court of General Seffions of the Peace was fuffered, however, to meet at *Worceſter* by adjournment, on the 21ſt of *November*, a circumſtance that, we ſhall find, the infurgents did not forget. The minds of the people, it was hoped, would be much changed with refpect to the courts abovementioned, from the meafures which had been adopted for leffening their bufinefs, by an act for rendering proceffes in law lefs expenfive. The defign of this act was to originate all perfonal civil actions before Juſtices of the Peace, with a view of finifhing them there. A trial however, was allowed before the higher courts, if the demand was difputed. The Houfe of Reprefentatives alfo paffed a bill for reducing the number

E 2   of

of terms of thefe courts, but the Senate referred it
over to their next affembling.

ANOTHER meafure on which the members of
the court, with very few exceptions, placed great
confidence, was, their addrefs to the people. In
this was very explicitly ftated the amount of the
federal and ftate debts, and the means propofed
for paying them. The neceffity of maintaining
the plighted faith of the commonwealth in the
publick fecurities was forcibly urged, upon principles of righteoufnefs and policy. All the taxes
fubfequent to the year 1780 were enumerated,
and the expenditures accounted for, as minutely
as the nature of the fubject would permit. The
falaries of the officers of government were fet
forth, and compared with thofe of the late province; and it was fhewn, that the whole annual expenfe of the government, being lefs than 19,000 l.
did not amount to fixteen pence upon a rateable
poll, exclufive of the proportion paid by the eftates. The neceffity of the major part governing
the community was held up againft the complaints of a number of parties, whofe projects being inconfiftent with each other, rendered it impracticable to adopt them. The cry for revifing
the conftitution was anfwered, by fhewing the
difficulties that were encountered in obtaining it ;
the

the little profpect there was of mending it ; and the improbability of finding at this time, that unuſual ſpirit of mutual condeſcenſion and domeſtick harmony, which accompanied the adoption of the frame of government, and which reſulted in a great meaſure, from a danger of foreign invaſion. The affiſtance of a paper medium was ſhewn to be ideal. Such a currency, it was obſerved, from experience, muſt depreciate, and that depreciation would be the ſource of miſery to the helpleſs part of the community, thoſe who were peculiarly under the guardianſhip of the legiſlature ; while unprincipled men only would grow rich, and the morals of the whole people become corrupt. The difficulties of the Commonwealth were attributed to the exceſſive uſe of foreign luxuries, to the decline of republican virtue, and to a ſpirit of unreaſonable jealouſy, and a complaining temper, which would render a theocracy itſelf a grievance. With reſpect to the burdens complained of by the diſcontented, the attention paid to their petitions, upon this ſubject, by different acts, was recited, and the conduct of the inſurgents was attributed to a wiſh to ſubvert all order and government. The different officers in the community, and the whole body of the people, were, therefore, called upon to oppoſe with fortitude and perſeverance, all attempts to impede

the

the courfe of juftice, and to render their own lives and property infecure; and, if any fhould be loft to all fenfe of juftice and virtue, they were affured, that the vengeance of an injured community, muft one day purfue and overtake them. This addrefs was ordered to be difperfed, and the feveral minifters of the Gofpel were requefted to read it to their congregations, on the enfuing thankfgiving day, or at a lecture to be purpofely appointed.

THUS, after paffing three different laws for eafing the burdens of the people, which were, an act for collecting the back taxes in fpecifick articles; an act for making real and perfonal eftate a tender in difcharge of executions and actions commenced in law, and an act for rendering law proceffes lefs expenfive; after appropriating one third of the proceeds of the impoft and excife duties for the exigencies of government; after attempting to enlighten the minds of the citizens, by an inftructive addrefs, and to reftore peace to the Commonwealth, by providing for the apprehending and trying of dangerous perfons; but, at the fame time, tendering indemnity to all the infurgents, the General Court rofe on the 18th of *November*, with reafonable expectations, that the people, if yet unfatisfied, would feek further alterations, by

the

the conftitutional means of inftructing their Reprefentatives, or by a change of officers in the future elections.

TO what caufes it was owing, that thefe expectations were not anfwered, it is difficult to con-
jecture. But, whether it was that the infurgents
really fuppofed their burdens to be intolerable,
and, by mifreprefentations had been led to think,
that they were contending againft a power which
would enflave them, if not effectually refifted ; or,
whether they thought themfelves to be a majority
of the people, as fome pretended, and fo vefted
with a fupreme power of altering whatever appeared to them to be wrong in the polity of the
country ; or whether their pride prevented them
from fubmitting to conditions of pardon, which a
confcioufnefs of their crimes evinced to be mild,
and difproportionate to treafonable offences ; or,
whether the plans of their leaders extending beyond the redrefs of grievances, did not admit of
any conciliatory meafures taking place—certain it
is, that the act of indemnity was treated with fo
much neglect, that fcarce a fingle perfon deigned
to accept of the benefits which it held up. The
lenient fyftem of government was attributed, not
to their humanity, but to their timidity and weaknefs ; whilft the fufpenfion of the privilege of the

E 4   writ

writ of *Habeas corpus*, with the other proceedings of the like nature, were carefully inferted, by thofe to whom they were dangerous, among the grievances of the people.

THE feffion of the General Court was immediately followed by a convention of delegates from feveral towns in the county of *Worcefter*. On the 23d of *November*, they fent out an addrefs to the people. In this they held up the right of the people to examine, cenfure and condemn the conduct of their rulers. They afferted, that the rulers of *Maffachufetts*, being many of them born to affluence, and perhaps the whole in eafy circumftances, had not been under advantages of feeling for the lefs wealthy ; and being at beft but fallible men, they had, as the convention apprehended, purfued a miftaken mode of policy. This was inftanced in the fmall value of real eftates. The ftopping of the courts of juftice was condemned as wrong, and as weakening their hands, and the people were entreated never more to attempt to obftruct thofe courts. They affected to hold up the embarraffments of the legiflature, as an apology for the grievances of the people not being redreffed in the way they could wifh, and cautioned them againft bringing government itfelf into contempt. They called upon

all

all electors to stand strictly to the exercise of their rights, assuring them that their delegates felt for their distresses, and would never forsake them while in the line of their duty : They concluded, with no small degree of vanity, that however they might suffer in their characters, persons or estates, if they could in the least degree contribute to restoring harmony to the Commonwealth, and to supporting the weight of a tottering empire, they should think themselves happy.

THE caution given in this address against bringing government into contempt, must have been exceedingly weakened in its operation, by the former part of it, wherein the right of condemning the publick rulers was asserted, and sentence accordingly passed upon them for mistaking the interests of the people. At any rate, the pacifick language of the convention did not seem to be thoroughly understood by their constituents ; for it happened in this case, as it did in most others, that their meeting was followed with additional tumults, instead of considerate measures on the part of the discontented. And, if the doings of publick bodies may receive a construction from the conduct of individuals which compose them, the circumstance of many members of conventions being afterwards found in the most atrocious acts

of

of fedition, and otherwife annoying the government, gives us reafon to fuppofe, that thofe affemblies, by this time, intended to fpeak in one language, and to be underftood in another.

ON the 21ft of *November*, when the Court of General Seffions of the Peace attempted to meet at *Worcefter*, according to adjournment, the feat of juftice was again found to be filled with armed men. The Juftices were obliged to open at a tavern ; and all the exertions of the Sheriff to procure them an entrance into the Court Houfe were in vain. As government, relying upon the late proceedings of the legiflature, took no meafures to oppofe a force, about 150 men in arms effectually difperfed the court, and prevented any bufinefs being done of a publick or private nature.

THE governour immediately on receiving the news of the procedure at *Worcefter*, iffued his orders as commander in chief ; wherein he obferved, that the very meafures which the General Court had adopted for removing the complaints of the malcontents, had been added to their catalogue of grievances, and furnifhed them with new pretences for complaining. He declared that he felt himfelf bound by the moft facred obligations of duty, to attempt, at all hazards, to crufh every

dangerous

dangerous oppofition to government, and he therefore called upon the Major Generals of the militia, immediately to fee that the feveral divifions were completely organized and equipped, and ready to take the field at the fhorteft notice.

IN purfuance of the refolution expreffed in thefe orders, the militia in *Middlefex* were directed to be in readinefs to march to *Cambridge*. Four regiments alfo were put into a like difpofition in *Effex* ; and the Sheriff of *Barnftable*, where fome fymptoms of uneafinefs began to appear, was directed to call upon the militia, to fupport the courts in that county, if neceffary.

NOTWITHSTANDING thefe military preparations, the militia were not actually marched out to fupport the Judicial Courts at *Cambridge*, which probably was occafioned by the peculiar circumftances of the infurgents at this time, when a degree of a conciliatory temper appeared to take place among them. An influential character in *Middlefex*, undertook to make an agreement with the leaders of that county, that no forces fhould appear on either fide, and wrote a letter to the Governour on this fubject, to their fatisfaction. But, the leaders in *Worcefter*, feeling more interefted to keep up the conteft, as they had broken the condition of the act of indemnity, and might

be

be left alone unleſs their brethren in the other
counties were perſuaded into the ſame temerity,
afterwards arrived, and, in a ſecret council, overruled this agreement. This deciſion was boldly
communicated to the abovementioned gentleman,
with explicit notice, that there would be a movement of the people. The plan was extenſive in its
operation, and more ſo in its deſign. A force was
actually ordered to march from *Worceſter* to *Cambridge*, to act in conjunction with the inſurgents
of *Middleſex*, and meſſengers were diſpatched to
a leader of *Briſtol* county, to march the people
thence, upon the ſame buſineſs. Reports were
alſo ſpread that troops were on the road from
Berkſhire and *Hampſhire*.

PURSUANT to this new ſcheme, a ſmall party
of *Middleſex* inſurgents, headed by *Oliver Parker*,
(*Job Shattuck*, their former Captain, coming in a
more ſecret manner, in order to avoid the appearance of breaking his agreement) marched into
the town of *Concord*. The ideas of this party appeared to be very wild, and not confined altogether to the ſtopping of the courts. Upon their
arrival, *Shattuck* proceeded in the night to *Weſ-
ton*, to get intelligence of the *Worceſter* forces ;
but, though they had begun their march, they
did not appear, and from this want of cooperation,

tion, the whole plan fell through. The infurgents at *Concord*, growing difheartened, fcattered
before any force could reach them. It ought not
to be omitted, that the anfwer from the leader in
Briftol, though too late to effect any meafures,
was, that the General Court had done fo much
for the people that they had determined not to
move.

THE leaders of the infurrections having thus
rejected the pardon which was held up to them by
the General Court, notwithftanding the great exertions which were made there to include them all
within it, the Governour and Council found themfelves neceffitated to exercife the higheft authority which was delegated to them by the legiflature, for fuppreffing the oppofition to government. Warrants were iffued for apprehending
the head men of the infurgents in *Middlefex*, as
being dangerous to the fafety of the Commonwealth, and for imprifoning them without bail or
mainprife. The execution 'of thefe warrants was
committed to the Sheriff of *Middlefex*, and others,
to whofe aid, a party of horfe, who had voluntarily affociated for the fupport of government, under Colonel *Benjamin Hichburn*, was ordered from
Bofton, early in the morning of the 29th of *November*. Thefe were joined by a party from
Groton,

Groton, under the command of Colonel *Henry Wood*, and the whole confifting of more than 100, proceeded immediately for *Concord*. On their arrival there, the *Groton* horfe, as being beft acquainted with the country, and leaft liable to excite an alarm from an unfamiliar appearance to the inhabitants, were difpatched to fecure the fubjects of the warrant. Thefe returned at night, with two prifoners, *Parker* and *Page*, but *Shattuck*, the principal leader, had taken an alarm and efcaped. Under this difappointment, at midnight, in the midft of a violent fnow ftorm, the whole party were ordered on to *Shattuck*'s houfe in *Groton*, where they did not arrive till late in the morning. Here they found that *Shattuck* had fled to the woods. A fearch was immediately commenced, and a judicious purfuit difcovered him to a party of a few perfons, led by Colonel *Wood* himfelf. *Shattuck* obftinately refifted, and was not taken until he had received feveral wounds, one of which was exceedingly dangerous, and which he returned, though without much injury. The three principal objects of the warrant being thus apprehended, the party returned to *Bofton*, on the next day but one after their departure, having pervaded the country for near fifty miles. The fhort time in which this excurfion

was

was performed with fo large a body, and the extreme feverity of the weather, rendered the execution of this fervice as honourable to the gentlemen who fubjected themfelves to it, as their motives in the undertaking were commendable.

THIS expedition was a very important event. By it the fword of government was unfheathed, while the obftinate fpirit of the malcontents, and the unlimited views of their oppofition, feemed to afford but little profpect of an accommodation on their part. The advantages derived from the capture of the prifoners were material. The heart of the infurrection in *Middlefex* was broken by fo fudden a ftroke, while the friends to good order received a confidence from the ftrength and fuccefs of their caufe. The perfonal fafety of the principal infurgents became precarious, and, could the attempts afterwards made for apprehending others of them have been attended with the fame fortunate iffue, the conteft would, probably, have been ended without further trouble or expenfe. But, they were afterwards, either guarded or fecreted by their followers, who feemed determined to oppofe themfelves boldly to the whole powers of the government.

WHILE this body of horfe were entering the county of *Middlefex,* another body of forty were
difpatched,

dispatched, under the command of Majors *Spooner*, and *Brimmer*, from *Roxbury*, into the county of *Worcester*, for the purpose of ascertaining the numbers and circumstances of the malcontents; and one of their principals owed his escape from them to misinformation alone. The alarm however, soon extended itself too far, for any further success by surprise, and this party were obliged to return, after reconnoitring the country, and collecting intelligence respecting the situation of the insurgents.

THE opposition to the Court of Sessions at *Worcester*, on the 21st of *November*, was evidently the renewal of an extensive system for opposing the administration of Justice. Previously to that day, all offenders stood upon a safe and honourable footing by the act of indemnity. But, that transaction, as must have been foreseen, threw the government into the dreadful dilemma, of either putting the courts of justice out of their protection, or of supporting them at the hazard of a civil war, and every unknown consequence which might follow an appeal to the sword. No sooner had the insurgents appeared at *Worcester*, than they attempted an unsuccessful cooperation with those at *Concord*, as we have mentioned, for the purpose of breaking up the courts at *Cambridge*.

But,

But the excursion of the light horse afterwards confined their operations to the courts at *Worcester*, which were to set the week following. With this intention, and perhaps for the better securing of their leaders, for whose safety they became exceedingly alarmed, the insurgents divided into several bodies, the principal party with *Shays*, their leader, retiring to the barracks at *Rutland*. Thus embodied they remained until *Sunday*, the 3d of *December*, when they began again to enter the town of *Worcester*.

IN the mean time, the Governour received letters from the Sheriff of *Worcester*, acquainting him of the intentions of the insurgents, and of the improbability of his collecting a sufficient force to oppose them. When this was first communicated to the Council, they advised, that orders should be sent to the Sheriff and Major General of that division, to use their utmost endeavours to support the courts; and letters were transmitted accordingly : But, upon a second consideration, a more extensive plan was agreed upon, and, instead of these orders ; the judges were advised to adjourn the courts to the 23d of *January* following. During the interval, it was judiciously conceived, the insurgent leaders would be exposed, and time would be afforded for the government

F

to

to eſtabliſh an effectual ſyſtem for the ſupport of the Judicial Courts. In the interim, while theſe courts were again put out of the way of the malcontents, the addreſs of the legiſlature was forwarded by expreſſes, with a view of enlightening the minds of the people.

THE inſurgents continued to enter the town of *Worceſter,* from the 3d to the 5th of *December,* notwithſtanding 170 men belonging to that place, turned out in arms to ſupport the courts, and a moſt violent ſnow ſtorm rendered travelling almoſt impracticable. But the courts met, and adjourned agreeably to the Governour's directions, to the 23d of *January.* The inſurgents neverthelefs, continued to aſſemble. *Shays,* with about 350 men, arrived from *Rutland;* and recruits came in from ſeveral quarters, until their numbers increaſed from 800 to 1000. Thus aſſembled, they placed guards at diſcretion, apprehended ſuch perſons as they pleaſed, among whom was one of the Judges; and billeted themſelves upon the inhabitants. No diſorders however, of an outrageous nature, took place.

THE object of oppoſition at *Worceſter* being removed, the inſurgents began to prepare for the continuance of their meaſures in *Hampſhire.* This
appears.

appears from the following addrefs, which was inferted in the Gazette of that county.

" *An* ADDRESS *to the People of the feveral towns in the county of* Hampfhire, *now at arms.*

" GENTLEMEN,

" WE have thought proper to inform you of fome of the principal caufes of the late rifings of the people, and alfo of their prefent movement, viz.

" 1ft. The prefent expenfive mode of collecting debts, which, by reafon of the great fcarcity of cafh, will of neceffity fill our gaols with unhappy debtors, and thereby a reputable body of people rendered incapable of being ferviceable either to themfelves or the community.

" 2d. The monies raifed by impoft and excife being appropriated to difcharge the intereft of governmental fecurities, and not the foreign debt, when thefe fecurities are not fubject to taxation.

" 3d. A fufpenfion of the writ of *Habeas corpus,* by which thofe perfons who have ftepped forth to affert and maintain the rights of the people, are liable to be taken and conveyed even to the moft diftant part of the Commonwealth, and thereby fubjected to an unjuft punifhment.

" 4th. The unlimited power granted to Juftices of the Peace and Sheriffs, Deputy Sheriffs, and

Conftables,

Conftables, by the Riot Act, indemnifying them
to the profecution thereof ; when perhaps, wholly
actuated from a principle of revenge, hatred and
envy.

"*Furthermore*, Be affured, that this body, now
at arms, defpife the idea of being inftigated by
Britifh emiffaries, which is fo ftrenuoufly propa-
gated by the enemies of our liberties : And alfo
wifh the moft proper and fpeedy meafures may be
taken, to difcharge both our foreign and domeftick debt.

"Per Order,

"DANIEL GRAY, *Chairman of the*
Committee, for the above purpofe."

AT the fame time appeared another publication, figned by a leader of the infurgents, and
purporting to come from the fame authority. If
it was the act of the people then affembled in
arms, it fhews their further fenfe of publick grievances ; if it was only founded on the authority of
the fubfcriber, it ferves to evince the confidence,
with which the unhappy tumults of the times infpired an obfcure individual to become a reform-
er, and to affume the fovereign right of contending for his object, by the fword.

THIS

THIS publication was as follows, viz.

" *To the Printer of the Hampſhire Herald.*

" SIR,

" IT has ſome how or other fallen to my lot to be employed in a more conſpicuous manner than ſome others of my fellow citizens, in ſtepping forth in defence of the rights and privileges of the people, more eſpecially of the county of *Hampſhire.*

" THEREFORE, upon the deſire of the people now at arms, I take this method to publiſh to the world of mankind in general, particularly the people of this Commonwealth, ſome of the principal grievances we complain of, and of which we are now ſeeking redreſs, and mean to contend for, until a redreſs can be obtained, which we hope, will ſoon take place ; and if ſo, our brethren in this Commonwealth, that do not ſee with us as yet, ſhall find we ſhall be as peaceable as they be.

" IN the firſt place, I muſt refer you to a draught of grievances drawn up by a committee of the people, now at arms, under the ſignature of *Daniel Gray,* chairman, which is heartily approved of ; ſome others alſo are here added, viz.

F 3 " 1ſt. The

" 1ft. The General Court, for certain obvious reafons, muft be removed out of the town of *Bofton.*

" 2d. A revifion of the conftitution is abfolutely neceffary,

" 3d. All kinds of governmental fecurities, now on intereft, that have been bought of the original owners for two fhillings, three fhillings, four fhillings, and the higheft for fix fhillings and eight pence on the pound, and have received more intereft than the principal coft the fpeculator who purchafed them—that if juftice was done, we verily believe, nay pofitively know, it would fave this Commonwealth thoufands of pounds.

" 4th. Let the lands belonging to this Commonwealth, at the eaftward, be fold at the beft advantage, to pay the remainder of our domeftick debt.

" 5th. Let the monies arifing from impoft and excife be appropriated to difcharge the foreign debt.

" 6th. Let that act, paffed by the General Court laft *June,* by a fmall majority of only feven, called the Supplementary Aid, for twenty five years to come, be repealed.

" 7th. The total abolition of the Inferiour Court of Common Pleas and General Seffions of the Peace.

" 8th.

" 8th. Deputy Sheriffs totally set aside, as a use-less set of officers in the community ; and Consta-bles who are really necessary, be empowered to do the duty, by which means a large swarm of lawyers will be banished from their wonted haunts, who have been more damage to the people at large, especially the common farmers, than the savage beasts of prey.

" To this I boldly sign my proper name, as a hearty wellwisher to the real rights of the people.
　　　　" THOMAS GROVER.
" *Worcester, December* 7, 1786."

THE insurgents still continued embodied, and alarming the whole Commonwealth, from the uncertainty of their next object.　Much talk was circulated, of their intending to march directly to *Boston,* in order to release *Shattuck,* and the other State prisoners confined there.　And this idea had impressed the Governour and Council so strongly, that they issued orders to Major General *Brooks,* to hold the *Middlesex* militia contiguous to the road, in readiness for action, and to dis-patch persons to watch the movements of the force at *Worcester.* But, the severity of the weath-er, and that want of enterprise in the insurgents, for which their obstinacy and perseverance was an inadequate substitute, entirely dissuaded them

F 4　　　　　　　　　from

from this attempt, if it ever formed a part of their
defigns. However, fo large a force, hanging, as
it were, over the heads of the citizens, uncertain
as to its direction, and liable to become predatory, from a want of means of fubfiftence, kept a
great part of the militia under military duty, and
deeply impreffed every man with concern. The
capital, where the prifoners were confined, was
under very unufual appearances. The feveral
alarm pofts were affigned to the citizens ; guards
were mounted at the prifon, and at the entrances
of the town ; and all things feemed to carry the
fhew of a garrifon. The confufion of the people
was greatly increafed alfo by the reports of the
difcontented, who magnified fome trifling ac-
cidents which happened in the excurfion of the
light horfe, and reprefented that enterprife, as a
moft bloody and cruel attack upon innocent citizens ; they held up the government as a tyranny
fubverting the liberties of the Commonwealth ;
they fpoke of themfelves as fufferers feeking the
redrefs of grievances, at the rifque of every thing ;
and they addreffed the pity and claimed the affiftance of the people, inafmuch as they were to be
equal fharers in the benefits for which they were
contending under fuch fufferings. In addition
to all this, the groffeft mifreprefentations were
made of the proceedings of government, and of
the characters of publick officers.   THE

THE continuance of the insurgent forces at *Worcester*, for any length of time, however desirable it might have been to their leaders, was not to be effected. Their numbers were considerable, and they had no other supplies than what a sudden departure from their several homes had allowed them to provide. To relieve the prisoners in *Boston* was not to be attempted ; and the courts were not to sit at *Springfield* until the 26th of the month. A separation therefore was unavoidable. Accordingly, a council of their leaders having been held, at which they concerted a plan for procuring a petition in their behalf, as we shall hereafter mention, they all left *Worcester* by the 9th of *December*. A large body of them with *Shays* their principal leader, retired by the way of *Rutland*, at which place they remained for some time.

THE retreat of these unhappy men, though less peaceable than their assembling, was attended with such distresses, as rendered them objects of pity. Some were actually frozen to death, and all of them were exposed to the inclemencies of the severest winter that had happened for many years. These difficulties were heightened by a scarcity of provisions, and, we may suppose, by an unwelcome reception among some persons, who

considered

considered them as the fomenters of sedition. Their cause during their whole expedition to *Worcester*, must have worn an unfavourable aspect in their own view. Indeed, this idea seemed to make a deep impression upon *Shays* himself, if he was sincere in a conversation which happened about this time, between him and a confidential officer of government. *Shays* was asked by this officer, who left it optional with him to answer the question or not, " Whether, if he had an opportunity, he would accept of a pardon, and leave his people to themselves ?" To which *Shays* answered, " Yes, in a moment." Upon a communication of this conversation to the Governour and Council, they empowered the officer to tell *Shays*, that, in case he would immediately leave the insurgents, and engage to conduct as a good citizen in future, he might be assured that he should be protected ; and, in case he should be convicted by any Judicial Court, of illegal proceedings, that he should receive a pardon from the Governour and Council. But this commission was afterwards returned, no opportunity having offered for the execution of it.

THE plan which the government had adopted on their part, being calculated to give time for the people to procure information of the measures
which

which the General Court had taken to redrefs their grievances, and to recollect themfelves ; it left the infurgents alfo at liberty, for a time, to defert or continue their violent proceedings. Of courfe, a very fmall force was neceffary to enable them to carry on their operations, if they chofe to maintain them. This they determined to do at *Springfield*, where, we may recollect, the Judicial Courts were adjourned to the 26th of *December*, by a refolve of the legiflature. *Shays* marched into that town, with other leaders of his party, who affembled about 300 malcontents, to oppofe the adminiftration of juftice. For this purpofe, they took poffeffion of the Court Houfe, and placed their guards according to the military ceremonies, which had by this time, become ufual and pretty generally known in cafes of fuch a nature. Their refpect, however, for the court, led to the decent mode of appointing a committee to wait on them with an order, couched under the humble appearance of a petition, requiring them not to proceed upon bufinefs. This fupplication was too well underftood, not to be inftantly granted, and fo both parties retired.

THIS good humoured decifion againft the ferious rights of the community, was however, the laft which the infurgents ever had it in their power er to negotiate. And they feemed aware, that further force might be neceffary, as on their return from *Worcefter*, their officers appointed a large committee to fuperintend the arrangement of the regiments in the county of *Hampfhire*, affigning to each member his particular divifion.

on the firft of *January*, the Governour and Council received information of the procedure at *Springfield*, and of there being the higheft probability, that the infurgents would appear at *Worcefter*, for the fame purpofe, on the 23d of that month. This was to ftride over the line which the government had diftinctly marked out for their defence. It might be faid to be paffing the Rubicon in this conteft; and to involve one or other of thefe confequences, that the whole conftitutional powers of the Commonwealth were to be proftrated at the feet of ufurpation and conqueft, or that the lives and fortunes of the adventurers were to be forfeited for a treafonable attempt againft their country. Under thefe circumftances, the Council did not hefitate to advife, that vigorous and effectual meafures fhould be taken to fupport the courts to be holden at *Worcefter*.

the mode of protecting the adminiftration of juftice, by calling on the *Poffe Comitatus*, was

found

found by repeated experience, to be ineffectual.
Such consequences had followed from exertions in
the publick cause, by threats against the lives of
those who were distinguished for their activity, and,
in one instance, by the secret firing of buildings,
that the friends of government in the disaffected counties, could no longer, unsupported, be
brought into the field against their neighbours,
at the risque of their property, and every comfort
of private life. It was therefore necessary, that
assistance should be given from different counties;
and it was accordingly advised by the Council,
that 700 men should be raised from the county
of *Suffolk,* 500 from *Essex,* 800 from *Middlesex,*
1200 from *Hampshire,* and 1200 from *Worcester;*
the whole amounting to 4,400 rank and file.
Two companies of artillery were ordered to be
detached from *Suffolk,* and a like number from
Middlesex. The troops from the three first named
counties, were ordered to rendezvous in the vicinity of *Boston,* on the 19th of *January;* those from
Hampshire at *Springfield,* on the 18th; those from
Worcester were to join the troops from the eastern
counties at the town of *Worcester;* and the whole
were to be raised for thirty days, unless sooner
discharged. The command of this respectable
force was given by his Excellency to Major
General *Benjamin Lincoln,* whose military reputation

tation and mildnefs of temper, rendered him doubly capacitated for fo delicate and important a truft.

BUT the raifing of this army, would have been as ineffectual a meafure for defending the Commonwealth, as any that had been purfued, had not fome fubftantial mode been adopted for fupplying it. The Commiffary and the Quartermafter General reprefented, that they had neither the articles neceffary for that purpofe, nor the money to purchafe them. Such was the low ftate of the publick treafury, that perhaps not a fingle company could have been maintained from that fource, if any funds had been appropriated for fuch ufes. The legiflature were not fitting, and had they been fitting, could not have laid a tax which would have raifed the monies in feafon. In this fituation, a number of gentlemen, from a conviction of the neceffity of maintaining good order, and from a confideration of the exigencies of government, voluntarily offered a loan to fupport the publick caufe. The Council advifed the Governour, to direct the Commiffary and Quartermafter General, to procure money or other articles from this loan, to an amount not exceeding 6000 l. and to recommend to the legiflature, upon their convening, to take effectual meafures for the fpeedy reimburfement of the fum fo borrowed.

IN

IN this manner was an army raifed, and afterwards marched into the field, by the Supreme Executive of the Commonwealth, in the recefs of the legiflatute. The General Court, at their laft fitting, had requefted the Governour ftill to perfevere in the exercife of fuch powers as were vefted in him by the conftitution, for preventing any attempts to interrupt the adminiftration of law and juftiee, and for enforcing due obedience to the authority and laws of government. Upon this requeft, and the inflexible perfeverance of the infurgents in their outrageous fyftem, the raifing of this army, the higheft act of conftitutional authority that is vefted in the Governour, appears to have been founded. And the meafure, we fhall find, was afterwards fully juftified, not only by the hearty approbation of the legiflature, but by its own confequences, in the reftoration of judicial proceedings, and the prefervation of the conftitution.

ON the 12th of *January*, while the militia were embodying, the Governour fent out an addrefs to the people of the Commonwealth. In this, the conduct of the infurgents, and the proceedings of the legiflature, with their requeft to him of the 24th of *October*, to ufe the powers vefted in him for enforcing obedience to the laws, were recited.

Agreeably

Agreeably to that requeſt, and to his own ideas of duty, the people were informed, that he had ordered a part of the militia to aſſemble in arms, for the purpoſe of protecting the Judicial Courts at *Worceſter*; of aiding the civil magiſtrate in executing the laws; of repelling all inſurgents againſt the government, and of apprehending all diſturbers of the publick peace.

IT was obſerved that the object of the inſurgents evidently was, to annihilate the preſent happy conſtitution, or force the General Court into meaſures repugnant to every idea of juſtice, good faith, and national policy. Succeſs in either caſe, muſt be deſtructive of civil liberty: And as it would be the reſult of force, undirected by moral principle, it muſt finally terminate in deſpotiſm, in the worſt of its forms.

MEN of principle, the friends of juſtice and of the conſtitution, were enjoined to unite, and by their union, if it ſhould be as firm as the inſurgents had been obſtinate, in trampling juſtice and the conſtitution under their feet, it was obſerved, a regular adminiſtration of law and juſtice would be eſtabliſhed, without the horrours of a civil war, which were ardently deprecated, and which the utmoſt endeavours would be uſed to prevent.
But

But unlefs force appeared, the greateft calamities feemed inevitable. If infurrection was to ftalk unoppofed by authority, fome confequences were fhewn ; and what, it was obferved, would be the end of fuch events, was known only to him, who could open the volume, and read the pages of futurity.

THE good people of the Commonwealth were therefore conjured, by every thing valuable in life, to cooperate with government in every necefary exertion for reftoring to the Commonwealth, that order, harmony and peace, upon which its happinefs and character fo much depended.

THE movements in raifing the army, could not but infpire the infurgents with ferious apprehenfions ; and they began upon a fyftem of policy, which they for a long time continued, of petitioning the government on the one hand, without relaxing their military exertions to overcome it on the other. When they were at *Worcefter*, they agreed upon a petition to the Governour and Council, which was to be fupported by as many towns as could be brought into the meafure. This petition, which had been once fent, but mifcarried, was again brought forward and prefented. It

G   contained,

contained, in substance, a request that the state prisoners might be liberated, and a general pardon again granted to all the insurgents ; that the Courts of Common Pleas might be adjourned to the next election ; and it then engaged for the peaceable conduct of the insurgents. The motive of petitioning was held up as arising not from the fear of death, or of any evils that might be placed in their way, but to prevent the cruelties and devastations of a civil war. But there did not appear any evidence that the person whose name was subscribed to this petition, was empowered to execute it, and it was dubious whether he himself signed it. Besides which, there was not a man present at the meeting where it was drawn, from the county of *Hampshire*, in behalf of the insurgents of which county, among others, it was presented. The Council therefore declared, that they could not consistently with their trust, attend to this paper, which they considered rather as an insult, than a petition, as it contained a threat, and not a sense of guilt in proceeding illegally : They therefore advised the Governour, to inform the bearer of this opinion ; at the same time observing, that whenever any citizen, or corporate body should prefer a petition, all due attention would be paid to it.

BUT

BUT the objections to this petition did not, at present, induce the insurgents to produce any other, better accommodated to the ideas of the Council. Their officers had previously issued their orders for the people immediately to assemble to support their rights, as it was termed, against the government. They therefore directed their attention, to a more authoritative mode of preferring their demands.

THE resolutions of the insurgents continuing thus hostile, the army of the state was put in motion, to support the Judicial Courts, under the command of General *Lincoln,* who received the following Orders from his Excellency the Governour.

" *Boston, January* 19, 1787.

"SIR,

" YOU will take the command of the militia, detached in obedience to my orders of the 4th instant. The great objects to be effected are, to protect the Judicial Courts, particularly those next to be holden in the county of *Worcester,* if the justices of the said courts should request your aid;—to assist the civil magistrates in executing the laws; and in repelling or apprehending all and every such person and persons as shall in a hostile manner, attempt or enterprise the destruc-

G 2   tion,

tion, detriment or annoyance of this Commonwealth; and also to aid them in apprehending the disturbers of the publick peace, as well as all such persons, as may be named in the state warrants, that have been, or shall be committed to any civil officer or officers, or to any other person, to execute.

" IF to these important ends, the militia already ordered out should, in your opinion, be incompetent, you will call on the Major Generals for further and effectual aid : And if you can rely on their attachment to government, you will in the first instance, call on the militia in the neighbourhood of your camp.

" I CANNOT minutely point out to you, the particular line you shall pursue in executing these orders : But would observe in general, that if, to answer the aforesaid valuable purposes, you should judge it necessary to march a respectable force through the western counties, you will in that case do it. This would give confidence to the well affected ; would aid and protect the civil officers in executing their duty, and would convince the misguided of the abilities of government, and its determination to pursue every legal, and constitutional measure for restoring peace and order to the Commonwealth.

" YOU

" you are to confider yourfelf, in all your military offenfive operations, conftantly, as under the direction of the civil officer, faving where any armed force fhall appear, and oppofe your marching to execute thefe orders.

" THAT I may be fully acquainted with all the proceedings of the armed force under your command ; and with all matters that refpect the great objects to be effected, you will pleafe to give me regular information by every poft : And for intermediate and neceffary intelligence, you will order the Quartermafter General to provide the neceffary expreffes.

" ON thefe attempts to reftore fyftem and order, I wifh the fmiles of heaven, and that you may have an agreeable command, the moft perfect fuccefs, and a fpeedy and fafe return ; and am with much efteem,

   " Sir,

    " Your moft obedient fervant,

     " JAMES BOWDOIN.

" Hon. Major General LINCOLN."

IN addition to the foregoing, the Council, upon letters from General *Lincoln* and General *Shepard* being laid before them by the Governour, advifed his Excellency, on the 24th of *January*, to give to General *Lincoln*, fuch further orders, as would enable him, in the fafeft and moft effectual manner, to apprehend, difarm and fecure, by all fitting ways and means, all perfons who, in a hoftile manner, fhould attempt or enterprife the deftruction, invafion, detriment, or annoyance of the Commonwealth ; and particularly all fuch bodies of armed men, as then were, or might be affembled in the counties of *Worcefter*, *Hampfhire*, *Berkfhire*, or elfewhere within this ftate, for the purpofe of oppofing the authority of the Commonwealth, founded on the laws and conftitution thereof. And orders were given by the Governour accordingly.

END OF THE FIRST PART.

HISTORY

OF THE

INSURRECTIONS, &c.

IN

MASSACHUSETTS, IN MDCCLXXXVI.

PART II.

EFORE we attend to the march of the army, it may not be improper to advert, for a moment, to the ſtate of parties, which by this time prevailed in the Commonwealth, and which greatly influenced the military operations, as well as all other meaſures, adopted for ſuppreſſing the inſurgents. In viewing theſe parties, it will ſtrike us with no ſmall ſurpriſe, that the cauſe of gov

ernment,

ernment, which was fo directly connected with
the adminiftration of juftice, and indeed with all
the effential principles of fociety, did not gain
greater numbers than what, from the progrefs of
the infurrections, and other circumftances, we
may fuppofe, really inlifted on its fide. But, as
has been mentioned, many perfons were led to
confider the fuccefs of their attempts to obtain a
redrefs of grievances, as depending upon the iffue
of the ftruggle refpecting the courts ; and doubt-
lefs were by thofe means induced to wink at an
abufe, which if taken by itfelf, they would have
viewed with abhorrence. The difcontented of
every clafs therefore, united at this important
ftage of the conteft, without much attention to
the difference between their feveral complaints,
or their propofed fyftems of reform. Many who
only wifhed for an alteration in the Judicial Courts,
were entangled with others, who intended if poffible, to prevent the adminiftration of juftice in any
way. Not a few of the more moderate in oppofition, who thought that they difcovered grievances in the mode of appropriating the impoft
and excife duties, or in the diftreffes of debtors,
and who wifhed for any reafonable alterations
which would quiet the minds of the people, were
carried down in the fame current of infurrection,

with

with thofe who were for annihilating both publick and private debts, and who aimed to revife or
extinguifh the conftitution. Men who in former years, had claffed themfelves on oppofite fides
of inveterate parties, were upon this occafion, to
be found together. There were thofe who had
been moft violently principled againft the revolution, and who hated the government as an effect of that event, uniting with flaming, but difappointed patriots, who had exerted all their a-
bilities to bring it about. Among the great body
of the difaffected, who were for altering the government, in order to enlarge the powers of the
people, there were alfo to be difcerned, many
who wifhed to carry popular meafures to fuch ex-
tremes, as to fhew their abfurdity, and demonftrate the neceffity of leffening the democratick
principles of the conftitution. The rage of the
times excited all thefe parties, from different, and
in fome inftances, from contrary motives, to attack the eftablifhed fyftem, without confidering,
if it were overthrown, upon whofe plan it could
be afterwards rebuilt. Thus was formed a che-
quered, but numerous body, fome have fuppofed
a third part of the Commonwealth, to aid, or at
leaft not to contend againft, the refiftance made
to the fitting of the courts.

TO

TO thefe however, was oppofed a ftill more powerful body, of which the men of property formed a material part. The holders of publick fecurities, and private creditors muft, from motives of fafety, have inlifted on this fide of the queftion. General principles of refpect to authority, and habits of obedience, had not yet loft their influence over many loyal and refpectable citizens. And the whole received a kind of cement from patriots, who faw the ufe which might be made of the commotions of the people by defigning men, for the purpofe of enflaving them ; and who too fenfibly recollected the blood and treafure, which had been expended in obtaining the conftitution, to renounce it for temporary evils. Befides thefe, we may reckon a third body of citizens, whom neither the idea of grievances on the one hand, nor the love of the conftitution on the other, could wholly draw off from a neutral ftation.

WITH the afcendancy or decline of thefe parties, the progrefs of the army, the ftruggles of the infurgents, and the proceedings of the government, were intimately connected.

ON the 19th of *January*, the army rendezvoufed at *Roxbury*, and reached *Worcefter* on the 22d, the day preceding the fitting of the Courts of
Common

Common Pleas and General Seffions of the Peace, in that place. This march was performed, with minute attention to the feelings of the inhabitants, and was calculated to infpire them with ideas of protection. It is fcarcely neceffary to obferve, that the Judicial Courts fet at *Worcefter*, without interruption from the infurgents, who, being un-equal to the refifting of fo refpectable a force, had turned their attention to a different object.

WHILE the government were quieting the low-er counties with even the appearance of their ar-my, a lefs flattering profpect opened in the weft. Previoufly to the marching of the troops from *Rox-bury*, orders had been given to General *Shepard*, to take poffeffion of the poft at *Springfield*. Here he accordingly collected about 900 men, and af-terwards reinforced them with the addition of near 200, all from the militia of the county of *Hamp-fhire*. The continental arfenal furnifhed a fuffi-cient number of field pieces, and fuch equip-ments, as were wanting for the men. To this refpectable poft the attention of the infurgents was directed in the firft inftance, and their ex-pectations were greatly raifed, from a hope of car-rying it previoufly to the arrival of the army under General *Lincoln*. Their movements therefore, were towards *Weft Springfield* on the one fide,

where

where about 400 men affembled under the command of *Luke Day* ; and towards the *Boſton* road on the other, where 1100 more were headed by *Shays* himſelf. Befides thefe, a party of about 400 from the county of *Berkſhire*, under the command of *Eli Parſons*, were ſtationed in the north pariſh of *Springfield*. The firſt of thefe parties undertook to ſtop and examine all paſſengers ; and cruelly wounded two perſons, who ſubmitted to their authority with reluctance.

THE inſurgents having collected thefe forces, which were refpectable from their numbers, and from the large proportion of old continental foldiers which they contained, *Shays*, on the 24th of the month, fent a meſſage to *Day*, informing him that he propoſed to attack the poſt at *Springfield* the next day, on the eaſt fide ; and defiring that *Day*'s forces might cooperate with him on the other. Whether *Day* found it really inconvenient to join in the attack on the 25th, or whether he was defirous of having the whole honour of General *Shepard*'s ſurrender, which was anxiouſly expected by the inſurgents, he was induced to delay the projected plan ; and his reply to *Shays*'s letter was, that he could not aſſiſt in the attack on the day propoſed, but would do it on the 26th. This anſwer however, was luckily intercepted by General

eral *Shepard,* and *Shays* took it for granted, that *Day* would cooperate with him, at the time he had mentioned. But inftead of this, *Day* only fent in an infolent fummons to General *Shepard,* acquainting him, that the body of the people af-fembled in arms, adhering to the firft principles in nature, felf prefervation, did in the moft pe-remptory manner, demand

" 1ft. That the troops in *Springfield* fhould lay down their arms.

" 2d. That their arms fhould be depofited in the publick ftores, under the care of the proper officers, to be returned to the owners at the ter-mination of the conteft.

" 3d. That the troops fhould return to their feveral homes upon parole."

on the fame day, *Shays* fent a petition, as it was termed, from *Wilbraham* to General *Lincoln,* in which he obferved, that from his unwillingnefs to be acceffory to the fhedding of blood, and from his defire of promoting peace, he was led to propofe, that all the infurgents fhould be indemnified, un-til the next fitting of the General Court, and un-til an opportunity could be had for a hearing of their complaints; that the perfons who had been taken by the government fhould be releafed, without punifhment; that thefe conditions fhould

be

be made fure by proclamation of the Governour :
On which the infurgents fhould return to their
homes, and wait for conftitutional relief from the
infupportable burdens under which they laboured. When this petition was written, General
Lincoln was two days march from *Springfield* ;
and if the object of it had been really pacifick,
fome time would have been allowed for an anfwer.

THE fituation of General *Shepard* and his party,
whom no one doubted the infurgents intended to
attack with all their force, was truly alarming.
His troops were decidedly inferiour in numbers
to thofe of the enemy ; and though he was pof-
feffed of artillery, yet he could derive little advantage from works thrown up on fuch a fudden
emergency. So doubtful was the iffue of an attack upon him, in the mind of General *Lincoln*,
and fo great was the chance of *Shays*'s gaining
importance and numbers from fuccefs, that on the
25th, General *Brooks* was called upon to march
with the *Middlefex* militia to *Springfield*, as early
as poffible.

WHILE affairs were in this critical ftate, General
Shepard, about 4 o'clock in the afternoon of the
25th, perceived *Shays* advancing on the *Bofton*
road, towards the arfenal where the militia were
pofted.

posted, with his troops in open column. Possessed of the importance of that moment, in which the first blood should be drawn in the contest, the General sent one of his aids with two other gentlemen, several times, to know the intention of the enemy, and to warn them of their danger. The purport of their answer was, that they would have possession of the barracks; and they immediately marched onwards to within 250 yards of the arsenal. A message was again sent to inform them, that the militia were posted there by order of the Governour, and of Congress, and that if they approached nearer, they would be fired upon. To this, one of their leaders replied, that *that* was all they wanted; and they advanced one hundred yards further. Necessity now compelled General *Shepard* to fire, but his humanity did not desert him. He ordered the two first shot to be directed over their heads; this however, instead of retarding, quickened their approach; and the artillery was at last, pointed at the centre of their column. This measure was not without its effect. A cry of murder arose from the rear of the insurgents, and their whole body was thrown into the utmost confusion. *Shays* attempted to display his column, but it was in vain. His troops retreated with precipitation to *Ludlow*, about ten

miles

miles from the place of action, leaving three of their men dead, and one wounded on the field.

THE advantages which the militia had in their power, both from the disorder of this retreat, which was as injudicious as the mode of attack, and from the nature of the ground, would have enabled them to have killed the greater part of the insurgents, had a pursuit taken place. But, the object of the commander was rather to terrify, than to destroy the deluded fugitives.

NOTWITHSTANDING this retreat, General *Shepard*, who had received no reinforcement, was under the strongest apprehensions of another attack from the whole body of the insurgents. Those on the west side of *Connecticut* river, under *Day*, had, from the intercepting of his answer to *Shays*'s letter, been wholly inactive in the attack ; and probably, were more irritated than dismayed at the defeat. The main army was more than a day's march distant ; and *Shays*'s party formed a junction with those under the immediate command of *Eli Parsons*, the *Berkshire* leader, at *Chickabee*, on the 26th, though this was attended with the loss of two hundred men, by desertion.

BUT the apprehensions of another attack at *Springfield*, were entirely allayed, by the arrival

of

of the army under General *Lincoln,* on the 27th of *January.* Four regiments, three companies of artillery, a corps of horfe, and a volunteer corps, appeared on that day at noon, and the remainder in the evening. The enemy were found pofted as we have defcribed, and *Day* had placed guards at the ferry houfe, and at the bridge over *Agawam* river, fo that all communications from the north and weft, by the ufual routes, were cut off.

NOTWITHSTANDING the fatigue of a march, performed in an uncommonly fevere winter, the army were ordered under arms at half paft three o'clock, the fame day on which they arrived. Four regiments, with four pieces of artillery, and the horfe, croffed the river upon the ice, while the *Hampfhire* troops, under the command of General *Shepard,* moved up the river, as well to prevent a junction of the party under *Shays,* who were on the eaft fide, with thofe under *Day,* on the weft, as to cut off the retreat of the latter. It was alfo a great object by this manœuvre, to encircle *Day,* with a force fo evidently fuperiour, as to prevent his people from firing, and thereby to avoid the fhedding of blood. Upon the appearance of the army on the river, the guard at the ferry houfe turned out, but forfook the pafs ; and after a fmall fhew of oppofition, near the

H   meeting

meeting houſe, retired in the utmoſt confuſion. This was attended with the flight of all *Day's* party, who eſcaped to *Northampton*, with the loſs of a very ſmall number, that were overtaken by the light horſe. The inſurgent forces under *Shays*, made no greater oppoſition, on the day following. When the army approached him, he immediately began a retreat, through *Southadley* to *Amherſt*, ſupplying the hunger of his men by plunder. A perſon who acted as an Adjutant in his party, was killed ; which happened, according to report, by the exceſſive agitation of his men, who miſtook their own rear guard, for an advanced party of General *Lincoln's* army.

THE appearance of things was exceedingly changed by the flight of the inſurgents from *Springfield*. The publick mind had been impreſſed with a generous anxiety for the fate of General *Shepard*, and the very reſpectable body of militia, which he had the honour to command. The iſſue of the attack upon them did not wholly allay this concern. The defeat, though deciſive, was not attended with ſuch loſs, as could diſcourage ſo large a body of men, as the inſurgents had collected, from further attempts, eſpecially if actuated by the motives which they pretended to hold out. The apprehenſions of the inhabitants

inhabitants had been alfo greatly raifed, from the various reports of the numbers and objects of the infurgents ; and more than all, from the aid which they affected to rely on, from fecret, but influential characters within the ftate, and the dif-contented of neighbouring governments. From fuch ideas, the meeting of the two armies in full force, at *Springfield*, was dreaded by all, in whofe minds the tranquillity of the country was the primary object.   But thefe fears wholly vanifhed, by the difperfing of the infurgent forces, and a fecurity naturally arofe from the flattering view of their broken and forlorn condition.   Orders were therefore immediately iffued for the return of the *Middlefex* militia, who, to the number of about two thoufand men, had begun their march, and were entering the county of *Worcefter*, which, it was at this time conjectured, might be protect-ed by the forces originally raifed.

THE march of this body however, was not with-out very beneficial effects to the publick caufe, which the friends of the infurgents were artfully undermining, with the fpecious pretext of pre-venting the fhedding of human blood.   Under this idea, they oppofed the raifing of men for the army, and endeavoured to turn the general fenfe of the people againft the meafures of government,

as

as precipitate and cruel. In *Middlesex*, an attempt was actually made, under the cover of this humane principle, to raise another convention, for devising means of settling the publick commotions, by other ways than those which the executive authority had directed. The motion of the troops under General *Brooks*, enabled him to adopt a decisive and spirited mode of conduct, which effectually stifled this baneful project in its infancy; and it demonstrated, what began to be questioned—that the repeated disappointments of the people of that county, in not marching, after very troublesome and expensive preparations for the field, had not destroyed their obedience to the commands of the government.

THE pursuit of *Shays* and his party, which commenced at two o'clock in the morning, was continued till the army reached *Amherst*, through which place, however, he passed before their arrival, on his way to *Pelham*, with the main body of his men. General *Lincoln*, finding the enemy out of his reach, directed his march to *Hadley*, the nearest place which could be found to afford a cover for his troops. Upon an examination of the houses at *Amherst*, it was discovered, that most of the male inhabitants had quitted them to follow the insurgents; and that ten sleigh loads of provisions
ions

ions had gone forward from the county of *Berk-shire*, for their ufe. Under fuch appearances, a ftrict prohibition was laid upon the remaining inhabitants, againft affording any fupplies to their deluded neighbours.

THE morning after the arrival of the army at *Hadley*, information was received, that a fmall number of General *Shepard*'s men, had been captured at *Southampton*, and that the enemy's party ftill continued there. The *Brookfield* volunteers confifting of fifty men, and commanded by Colonel *Baldwin*, were fent in fleighs, with 100 horfe, under the command of Colonel *Crafts*, to purfue them. They were foon found to confift of eighty men with ten fleighs, and at twelve o'clock the fame night were overtaken at *Middle-field*. They had quartered themfelves in feparate places; and about one half of them, with one *Luddington* their captain, being lodged in a houfe together, were firft furrounded. It was a fingular circumftance, that among the government's volunteers, happened to be General *Tupper*, who had lately commanded a continental regiment, in which *Luddington* had ferved as a Corporal. The General, ignorant of the character of his enemy, fummoned the party to furrender. How aftonifhed was the Corporal at receiving this fummons,

in

in a voice to which he had never dared to refuse
obedience ! A momentary explanation took place,
which but heightened the General's commands.
Refiftance was no longer made, the doors were
opened, and a furrender was agreed to.   By this
time, the reft of the party had paraded under
arms, at the diftance of 200 yards, where they
were met by a number of men prepared for their
reception.   Both fides were on the point of firing, but, up ֗ an artful reprefentation of the
ftrength of the government's troops, the infurgents laid down their arms, and fifty nine prifoners, with nine fleigh loads of provifions, fell into
the hands of the conquerors, who returned to the
army on the day following.

THE whole force of the infurgents having taken
poft on two high hills in *Pelham*, called eaft and
weft hills, which were rendered difficult of accefs
by the depth of the fnow around them, General
Lincoln, on the 30th of *January*, fent a letter directed to Captain *Shays*, and the officers commanding the men in arms againft the government
of the Commonwealth, as follows :

" WHETHER you are convinced or not of
your errour in flying to arms, I am fully perfuad-
ed that before this hour, you muft have the ful-
leſt

left conviction upon your own minds, that you are not able to execute your original purposes.

" YOUR resources are few, your force is inconsiderable, and hourly decreasing from the disaffection of your men; you are in a post where you have neither cover nor supplies, and in a situation in which you can neither give aid to your friends, nor discomfort to the supporters of good order and government—Under these circumstances, you cannot hesitate a moment to disband your deluded followers. If you should not, I must approach, and apprehend the most influential characters among you. Should you attempt to fire upon the troops of government, the consequences must be fatal to many of your men, the least guilty. To prevent bloodshed, you will communicate to your privates, that if they will instantly lay down their arms, surrender themselves to government, and take and subscribe the oath of allegiance to this Commonwealth, they shall be recommended to the General Court for mercy. If you should either withhold this information from them, or suffer your people to fire upon our approach, you must be answerable for all the ills which may exist in consequence thereof."

TO this letter the following Answer was received.

H 4   " Pelham,

"*Pelham, January 30th*, 1787.

"To General LINCOLN, commanding the government troops at *Hadley*.

"S I R,

"T H E people affembled in arms from the counties of *Middlefex, Worcefter, Hampfhire* and *Berkfhire*, taking into ferious confideration the purport of the flag juft received, return for anfwer, that however unjuftifiable the meafures may be which the people have adopted, in having recourfe to arms, various circumftances have induced them thereto. We are fenfible of the embarraffments the people are under; but that virtue which truly characterizes the citizens of a republican government, hath hitherto marked our paths with a degree of innocence; and we wifh and truft it will ftill be the cafe. At the fame time, the people are willing to lay down their arms, on the condition of a general pardon, and return to their refpective homes, as they are unwilling to ftain the land, which we in the late war purchafed at fo dear a rate, with the blood of our brethren and neighbours. Therefore, we pray that hoftilities may ceafe, on your part, until our united prayers may be prefented to the General Court, and we receive an anfwer, as a perfon is gone for that purpofe. If this requeft may be complied with,

government

government fhall meet with no interruption from the people ; but let each army occupy the poft where they now are.

"DANIEL SHAYS, *Captain.*"

ON the next day, three of the infurgent leaders came to Head Quarters with the following letter.

"*The Honourable General* LINCOLN.

"S I R,

" AS the officers of the people, now convened in defence of their rights and privileges, have fent a petition to the General Court, for the fole purpofe of accommodating our prefent unhappy affairs, we juftly expect that hoftilities may ceafe on both fides, until we have a return from our legiflature.

" YOUR Honour will therefore be pleafed to give us an anfwer.

" Per order of the committee for reconciliation.

"FRANCIS STONE, *Chairman.*
"DANIEL SHAYS, *Captain.*
"ADAM WHEELER.

" *Pelham, January* 31, 1787."

TO this the following Anfwer was fent.

" *Hadley,*

" *Hadley, January* 31*ſt,* 1787.

" GENTLEMEN,

" YOUR requeſt is totally inadmiſſible, as no powers are delegated to me which would juſtify a delay of my operations. Hoſtilities I have not commenced.

" I HAVE again to warn the people in arms a-gainſt government, immediately to diſband, as they would avoid the ill conſequences which may enſue, ſhould they be inattentive to this caution.

" B. LINCOLN.

" *To* FRANCIS STONE,
      DANIEL SHAYS,
      ADAM WHEELER."

THESE communications on the part of the in-ſurgents, were backed by committees from diſaf-fected towns, who began to looſe confidence in the ſtrength of their party, and therefore thought it time to attempt an accommodation. This they carried on conveniently enough, under the pre-tence of preventing the effuſion of blood, without betraying the true motives of their application. The anſwer which was given them, though prob-ably not very conſonant to their feelings, could not have been without its effects. They were adviſed to exert their abilities, to withdraw the

men

men belonging to their several towns, from the body of the insurgents, which would effectually secure them from harm, and destroy the unlawful combination, that alone had endangered the lives of the people on either side.

DURING these negotiations between the army and the insurgents, the time arrived for the assembling of the legislature. But such was the general confusion of affairs throughout the state, that a sufficient number of representatives could not be collected until the third of *February*, which was the fourth day after the time of adjournment. The Court then acquainted the Governour, that they were prepared to receive his communications, and he addressed them by a speech from the chair, which contained a retrospective account of the malcontents, as to their views and proceedings, and of the measures which the government had adopted to oppose them. Vigour and energy were strongly recommended, as the proper means of crushing so unprovoked an insurrection, while a want of them might draw on the evils of a civil war. A reimbursement of the monies borrowed for raising the militia, was also advised, with an adequate provision, for defraying the general expense of the campaign, and several secondary measures for the same purpose.

AFFAIRS

AFFAIRS had been brought to such a crisis, that there was no room left for the legislature to waver in their opinions, or to delay their measures. The whole community were in an alarm, and the appeal to the sword was actually made. One army or the other was to be supported, and there could be no hesitation in the mind of any reasonable man, which it ought to be. On the next day therefore, a declaration of Rebellion was unanimously passed in the Senate, and concurred by the lower House. This however was accompanied by a resolve, approving of General *Lincoln*'s offer of clemency to the privates among the insurgents, and empowering the Governour in the name of the General Court, to promise a pardon, under such disqualifications, as should afterwards be provided, to all privates and noncommissioned officers, that were in arms against the Commonwealth, unless excepted by the general officer commanding the troops, upon condition of their surrendering their arms, and taking and subscribing the oath of allegiance, within a time to be prescribed by the Governour.

ON the same day, an answer was also sent to the Governour's speech. In this the Court informed his Excellency of their entire satisfaction, in the measures which he had been pleased to take for

subduing

subduing a turbulent spirit, that had too long in-
sulted the Government of the Commonwealth;
and congratulated him on the success which had
attended them. They earnestly entreated him
still to continue them, with such further constitutional measures, as he might think necessary,
to extirpate the spirit of rebellion; for the better
enabling of him to do which, they thought it necessary to declare that a rebellion existed. They
assured him of the most effectual measures being
used, for paying the army, and reimbursing the
monies which had been generously advanced for
their support. They accorded with the Governour, in his idea of the propriety of vigorous
measures; and requested him, in case the numbers of the militia who were inlisted should be
too small, or the time for which they were to
serve, too short, that he would increase them, and
continue them in service, until the objects in
view should be completely accomplished. They
subjoined, that they would vigorously pursue every measure, which would be calculated to support the constitution, and would continue to' redress any real grievances, if such should be found
to exist.

AGREEABLY to the assurances contained in this
address, the legislature passed an act, for appropriating

priating 40,000 l. of the impoſt and exciſe duties, for reimburſing the loan of monies, borrowed for ſuppreſſing the rebellion : And they unanimouſly paſſed a reſolve, approving of the ſpirited conduct of General *Shepard*, and the militia of his diviſion, in their defence of the arſenal at *Springfield*, againſt the attack of the inſurgents.

THE accounts of the numbers, reſources and objects of the malcontents continued to be exceedingly variant ; and from the meaſures of government, it is probable, that their real ſtrength differed greatly at different times. When they were diſperſed at *Springfield*, ſuch was the hopeleſs proſpect before them, that 2000 militia who were marching to aid the army, were diſcharged by the commanding officer, as we have mentioned, for want of employment. But upon their taking poſt at *Pelham*, their importance increaſed to ſuch a degree, as to produce a further requiſition for men, and the Governour accordingly iſſued his orders, for 2600 of the militia in the middle counties, to take the field.

THE Petition mentioned in the letter from *Shays* and his aſſociates, at *Pelham*, was in fact preſented to the Legiſlature, and was conceived in the following terms.

" *Commmon-*

" *Commonwealth* of *Maffachufetts.*

" To the Honourable the SENATE, and the
Honourable HOUSE of REPRESENTATIVES, in
General Court affembled at their next Seffion.

" *A* PETITION *of the* OFFICERS *of the counties
of* Worcefter, Hampfhire, Middlefex, *and*
Berkfhire, *now at arms,*

" HUMBLY SHEWETH,

" THAT your petitioners being fenfible that we
have been in an errour, in having recourfe to arms,
and not feeking redrefs in a conftitutional way ;
we therefore heartily pray your honours, to over-
look our failing, in refpect to our rifing in arms,
as your honours muft be fenfible, we had great
caufe of uneafinefs, as will appear by your redreffing many grievances, the laft feffion ; yet
we declare, that it is our hearts defire, that good
government may be kept up in a conftitutional
way ; and as it appears to us, that the time is near
approaching, when much human blood will be
fpilt, unlefs a reconciliation can immediately take
place, which fcene ftrikes us with horrour, let
the foundation caufe be where it may :

" WE therefore folemnly promife, that we will
lay down our arms, and repair to our refpective
homes,

homes, in a peaceable and quiet manner, and fo remain, provided your honours will grant to your petitioners, and all thofe of our brethren who have had recourfe to arms, or otherways aided or affifted in our caufe, a general pardon for their paft offences.—All which we humbly fubmit to the wifdom, candour and benevolence of your honours, as we in duty bound fhall ever pray.

"FRANCIS STONE, *Chairman of the committee for the above counties.*

" Read and accepted by the officers.

" *Pelham, January* 30, 1787."

BY this petition it appears, that the infurgent officers intended to open a treaty, and to avail themfelves of the force which they had collected, amounting by general computation to 2000 men, for the purpofe of obtaining advantageous terms. And it became a prevailing fentiment, that a regard for the fafety of their leaders, fome of whom had been partly compelled to accept of their appointments, held the armed body together at *Pelham.* But the court, whofe decifion upon this petition was not concluded till the 8th of *February,* did not feem inclined to encourage fuch a treaty; as appears from the following proceedings.

" A PAPER

" A PAPER called a Petition from the officers
of the counties of *Worcester, Hampshire, Middlesex* and *Berkshire*, now at arms, and signed by
Francis Stone, chairman of the committee from
the above counties, and addreffed to the General
Court, was read :

" Whereupon *Voted*, That the faid paper cannot be fuftained :

" *First*, Becaufe thofe concerned therein, openly avow themfelves to be at arms, and in a ftate
of hoftility againft the government ; and for this
reafon alone, the faid paper would be unfuf-
tainable, even if the tenour of the application had
difcovered a fpirit fuitable to the object of it.

" *Secondly*, Becaufe it does not appear, what
officers or how many are reprefented in the faid
paper, or that the faid *Stone* had authority from
any officers whatever, to make the application by
him fubfcribed.

Thirdly, Becaufe the applicants, although they
call themfelves petitioners, and acknowledge an
" errour," yet confider that errour only as " a failing," and attempt, at leaft in part, to juftify
themfelves therein.

" *Fourthly*, The faid applicants appear to view
themfelves on equal, if not better ftanding than
the legiflature, by propofing " a reconciliation."

I   " *Fifthly*,

" *Fifthly*, They appear to threaten the authority and government of the Commonwealth, with great effusion of blood, unlefs this " reconciliation" can immediately take place.

" *Sixthly*, They implicitly declare their determination to continue in arms, unlefs all who now are, and who have been in a ftate of open war with the government, including thofe who have been apprehended, and are now in cuftody, as well as all others who have any way aided or affifted in their caufe, can have another full pardon granted for all offences, in addition to that which they have fo lately defpifed.

" *Seventhly*, If the paper prefented had been a proper petition, fubfcribed by the perfons who defire a pardon, and expreffive of a due fenfe of their crime, with proper refolutions of amendment, yet their engagements could not be depended on, as their caufe has been fupported by a multitude of falfehoods ; and as no engagements can be more folemn than thofe made by the leaders of the rebels in the county of *Middlefex*, on the week before the Judicial Courts fat laft in the faid county, that they would not take any meafures to obftruct the fitting of the faid courts ; which engagements were fo far regarded, as to induce the commander in chief, to write counter
orders

orders to a confiderable part of the militia, whom he had ordered to be detached; and yet thofe engagements were on the next day violated."

THE infurgents, however, did not wait at *Pelham* for the refult of their petition to the legiflature. One of their leaders requefted a private conference with an officer of the army, upon the pretended fubject of a promife of pardon to all the principals of his party. This was granted; and took place on the 3d of *February*. But, while the conference was holding, and while the attention of the army was attracted by it, the infurgents withdrew themfelves from *Pelham*, and marched to *Peterfham*. Whether this was occafioned by their poft being reconnoitred the preceding day, or by a wifh of being fituated more advantageoufly for a fupply of provifions, and a communication with their friends, is uncertain. Their movement was remarkable, for its being the laft time they appeared in any confiderable force; and for its having given rife to one of the moft indefatigable marches, that ever was performed in *America*.

INFORMATION of the enemy's being in motion, was brought to General *Lincoln*, at *Hadley*, at twelve o'clock the fame day on which it happened. But it was then fuppofed, to have been on-

ly

ly a removal from the weſt to the eaſt hill in *Pel-ham*. Orders however, were iſſued for the army to be in readineſs to march, with three days proviſions, at a moment's warning. At ſix o'clock undoubted intelligence was received, that the inſurgents had really left their poſt, and gone eaſtward. In two hours from this, the army proceeded after them. Nothing more than the uſual inclemency of the ſeaſon oppoſed their march until two o'clock in the morning, by which time they had advanced as far as *Newſalem*. Here a violent north wind aroſe, and ſharpened the cold to an extreme degree ; a ſnow ſtorm accompanied, which filled the paths ; the route of the army lying over high land, expoſed the ſoldiers to the full effects of theſe circumſtances, while on their way ; and, the country being thinly ſettled, did not afford a covering for them within the diſtance of eight miles. Being thus deprived of ſhelter by the want of buildings, and of refreſhment—by the intenſeneſs of the cold, which prevented their taking any in the road, their only ſafety lay in cloſely purſuing a march, which was to terminate at the quarters of the enemy. They therefore advanced the whole diſtance of thirty miles, ſubject to all theſe inclemencies, without halting for any length of time. Their front reached *Peterſham* by nine o'clock in the morning, their rear being five miles diſtant.

IT

IT has been thought by some, that in this state of the troops under government, had the insurgents possessed any considerable degree of vigilance or discipline, they might have given them a severe check, if not a total defeat. These seeming advantages arose from unforeseen circumstances, and from causes which no human power could control. The opposers of government had, at this moment, all the advantages which they could ever expect to enjoy. Their men had been lodged in warm houses, and were capable of entering into action with alertness, whilst their pursuers were suffering exceedingly from the cold, and were greatly worn down with fatigue. The general however, advanced with the utmost confidence of success, being well acquainted with every inch of ground he had to tread in his approach to the town ; and having his flanks covered from any sudden impression, by a very deep snow, so crusted as nearly to bear a man. He knew therefore that he could not be annoyed, but in front, in a very narrow sled path, which, having a part of his artillery advanced, he could command to a very great distance. If the insurgents possessed advantages, they were lost by an idea of their own security, from which they were first awakened by an advanced guard led into the town by Colonel *Haskel.* A company of artillery with two pieces

I 3   of

of cannon immediately followed, and the whole body of the army was brought up as early as pofsible. Nothing feemed to be more foreign from the expectations of the infurgents, than a purfuit through fo many difficulties, and in fo fhort a time. The furprife was therefore complete, and they inftantly evacuated the houfes, thronging into a back road which leads towards *Athol.* Through this they quitted the town in great confufion, fcarcely firing a gun. They were purfued about two miles, and one hundred and fifty of them were taken prifoners. Many retired to their own homes, and the reft, including all their principal officers, fled into the ftates of *Newhampfhire, Newyork* and *Vermont.* The privates among the prifoners, after being difarmed, and taking the oath of allegiance, received paffports to return to their feveral towns.

THE news of the arrival of the army at *Peterfham,* and of their fuccefs in difperfing the infurgents, reached the court by a meffage from the Governour, on the 6th of *February.* It gave great fupport to the friends of the government, who were, after this, no longer doubtful of the fenfe and determination of the people to maintain the publick caufe. But notwithftanding the difabled fituation of the malcontents, the court, at

firft,

firft, did not incline to countermand the orders for raifing the 2600 men; judging it the moft certain means of preventing bloodfhed, to appear with a decided fuperiority of force. Thefe orders however, were neceffarily fuperfeded, upon further information from the army, which induced the two Houfes, on the 8th of *February*, to refolve that a number of men not exceeding 1500, fhould be inlifted to ferve for four months, unlefs fooner difcharged. And they, at the fame time, requefted the Governour to iffue a proclamation, offering a reward not exceeding 150 l. for apprehending either of the leaders in the rebellion, and to write to the Governours of other ftates, to requeft them to iffue fimilar proclamations for the fame purpofe. The legiflature alfo, in their anfwer to the Governour, expreffed the high fenfe which they entertained of the ardour and zeal of General *Lincoln*, and the army under his command, in performing the march from *Hadley* to *Peterfham*, with only a momentary halt, and in repelling the rebels; and defired that it might be communicated to them.

THE routing of the infurgents at *Peterfham*, changed the mode of their carrying on their conteft. After this, it was in vain for them to attempt an oppofition to the army, by a collected

I 4 force.

force. They therefore determined to harrafs the inhabitants in fmall parties by furprife. This mode of offence was attended with rancour, robbery and murder. The evils of war had before been gathered and confined to one fpot; but they were, by thefe means, fcattered through the whole weftern part of the ftate.

THE difqualifications which were to be the conditions of indemnity to the rebels, could not be brought to a conclufion, until the 16th of *February*. A fubject fo new and unaffayed in *Maffachufetts*, as that of disfranchifing the citizens, was neceffarily attended with many perplexities. This was the point at which the future character of the offenders, and of their caufe, was to be fixed in the publick opinion. The effect of their punifhment greatly depended upon the affent of mankind to the juftice of it; and this was to be obtained, only by the exacteft proportion between the penalty and the crime. It was eafy to forefee, that if the former exceeded the moft moderate limits, numbers, inftead of being deterred at the fate of the culprits, would forget or excufe their crimes, and become advocates for them, as the oppreffed victims of power. To punifh in fuch a cafe, was a truly critical tafk; and delay was the leaft inconvenience which could happen, in

settling

settling a measure, that scarce any length of time would have been mispent in considering. The substance of these conditions, which extended only to noncommissioned officers and privates, finally was, that the offenders, having laid down their arms, and taken the oath of allegiance to the Commonwealth, should keep the peace for three years ; and during that term, should not serve as jurors, be eligible to any town office, or any other office under the government ; should not hold or exercise the employments of schoolmasters, innkeepers, or retailers of spiritous liquors, or give their votes, during the same term of time, for any officer civil or military, within the Commonwealth : Unless they should, after the first day of *May*, A. D. 1788, exhibit plenary evidence of their having returned to their allegiance and kept the peace, and of their possessing an unequivocal attachment to the government, as should appear to the General Court, a sufficient ground, to discharge them from all or any of these disqualifications.

THE Governour was empowered to dispense with the whole, or any part of these conditions of indemnity, to all such privates as, having borne arms against the government, voluntarily took up arms in its support, previously to the first of *February ;*

February ; and to such as, agreeably to the pro-
posals of General *Lincoln* of the 29th and 30th
of *January*, voluntarily came in, surrendered their
arms, and took and subscribed the oath of allegiance, within three days. The persons absolutely
excepted from the indemnity, were included in
the following descriptions.—Such as were not
citizens of the state ; such as had been members
of any General Court in the state, or of any state
or county convention, or had been employed in
any commissioned office, civil or military ; such
as, after delivering up their arms, and taking the
oath of allegiance during the rebellion, had again
taken and borne arms against the government ;
such as had fired upon, or wounded any of the
loyal subjects of the Commonwealth ; such as had
acted as committees, counsellors, or advisers to
the rebels ; and such as, in former years, had been
in arms against the government, in the capacity
of commissioned officers, and were afterwards
pardoned, and had been concerned in the rebellion.

THE unanimity which had prevailed in the General Court during the session, was interrupted at
the passing of this law. The friends to lenient
measures, by this time, began again to advance
their sentiments. Petitions from more than twenty

ty towns had appeared, to requeſt the liberation of the ſtate priſoners, and, in ſome inſtances, the recal of the ſtate's army, under the humane idea of preventing the ſhedding of blood. This party. therefore, took the preſent opportunity, to inter-cede for perſons whom they could not juſtify ; and to mitigate a puniſhment, which the crimin-al perſeverence of the rebels had made it impoſ-ſible further to delay or avoid. It was urged, that the government was put beyond danger ; and to purſue the publick enemy further than the publick ſafety directed, was for them to diſcover paſſion and reſentment, which no government ought to entertain. That the ſooner a ſpirit of conciliation was introduced among individual citizens, who, from taking different ſides, had be-come either elated with ſuccefs, or mortified from the want of it, the ſooner publick tranquillity would be reſtored, and the government be eſtab-liſhed in the affections of the people. That, to effect this great end, caution alſo ſhould be uſed not to render thoſe perſons deſperate, who had been led into the rebellion from miſinformation and ignorance, which was the misfortune of a large number of honeſt and ſubſtantial citizens. That odious diſtinctions would have this unhap-py effect, and the beſt characters might be ſhut out, rather than ſubmit to terms, which they

ſhould

should think beyond their crimes ; while bad men, who would comply with them only in appearance, might avail themselves of such terms to the injury of the Commonwealth. That the rebellion, however unjustifiable, had in fact engaged large numbers on its side, and good policy evidently directed, rather to recal them to the bosom of their country, than to weaken the state by their final expulsion. In answer to these arguments, the magnitude of the crime, and the nature of the disqualifications, were urged. Some test, it was said, ought evidently to be required of persons who had taken the last means of resisting the government, and overturning the constitution : And, whenever repentance appeared, means were provided for the total exculpation of the offenders, after the expiration of a very few months.

THE advocates for the insurgents had so often pledged themselves for their reformation, on condition of lenient measures being adopted ; and these had so often failed of effecting this desirable purpose, that their observations were at length less attended to than usual, and possibly less than they deserved. And it was unfortunate to their influence, that, in this instance, as had before been the case, the conduct of the rebels flatly contradicted every argument which they could raise in their favour.

favour. While the difqualifying bill was under debate in the lower houfe, and at the moment a refpectable member of the minority was endeavouring to foften the conditions, letters were received from General *Lincoln,* who, by that time, had proceeded into the county of *Berkfhire,* ftating the obftinacy and malignant conduct of the rebels in fuch a manner, as literally to fhut his mouth: And the bill was carried.

THE rebels having fled in various directions, when the army arrived at *Peterfham,* the General, after difmiffing three companies of artillery, and ordering two regiments to *Worcefter,* directed his attention towards *Northfield,* in the neighbourhood of which place, many of the fugitives had taken fhelter. But, an exprefs arrived from Major General *John Patterfon,* the commander of the militia in *Berkfhire,* which occafioned an alteration in his plan.

WHILE the army were on their march, the infurgents in that county who had not joined their main body under *Daniel Shays,* endeavoured to fupport their caufe, and diftract the attention of government, by appearing under arms in their own neighbourhood. The friends to good order alfo, were not inactive upon the occafion.

occasion. It was conjectured by them, that the malcontents, from a want of resources, would be dispersed by the army under General *Lincoln*; and, in that case, they supposed it more than probable, that *Shays* would seize on the heights which lie between the counties of *Hampshire* and *Berkshire*, where strong posts were to be found, and the passes easily defended; and, thus situated, would draw the means of his subsistence, from the towns well affected to government, which abounded in plenty; securing also, perhaps, the most important characters, as hostages. They therefore, voluntarily associated to the number of about 500, for the defence of themselves, and of the publick cause. In this body, most of the respectable inhabitants of the county were to be found, and men of the first importance submitted to the duty of the ranks. The insurgents began to assemble at *West Stockbridge*, under one *Hubbard*, who posted himself at the meeting of three roads, for the convenience probably, of collecting men. Here he drew together about 150 or 200 of the disaffected. It was conceived to be absolutely necessary, to disperse this party, before their numbers should grow more respectable. The whole body of the friends to government were ordered to march for this purpose, in several directions, which the roads naturally pointed out,

and

and which would enable them to furround the
enemy. On the approach of an advanced party,
confifting only of thirty feven infantry, and feven
gentlemen on horfeback, they were fired upon by
Hubbard's fentries ; and the whole of his men
were inftantly put into good order, and commanded to fire. But, fuch was the effect of their
fituation upon their minds, that they ftaggered
apparently. Timely advantage was taken of their
panick : A gentleman* whom they well knew,
rode up to their front, and directed them to lay
down their arms, which many of them complied
with, whilft others fled. A firing took place between fcattering parties on both fides, by which
two of the infurgents were wounded. Eighty
four of them, among whom was *Hubbard* himfelf,
were made prifoners ; and moft of thefe, after being difarmed, were admitted to the oath of allegiance, and fent home. The exprefs informed,
that the infurgents had afterwards collected, in
the town of *Adams* ; but, upon General *Patterfon*'s approach, they feparated, with an intention
of collecting again at *Williamftown*. Here alfo,
upon his appearing, they were again fcattered.
That there feemed, neverthelefs, fuch a difpofition

---

* The Hon. THEODORE SEDGWICK, Efq; the Speaker of
the prefent Houfe of Reprefentatives.

tion in the infurgents to embody, in order to prevent the fitting of the courts, and fuch numbers
were actually upon their march towards *Wafh-
ington*, under the direction of a Major *Wiley*, as
made his fituation unfafe, and he earneftly requefted affiftance from the main army.

UPON this information, General *Lincoln* directed his march immediately for the county of
Berkfhire, paffing through the towns of *Amherft*,
Hadley, *Chefterfield*, *Partridgefield* and *Worthing-
ton*, into *Pittsfield* ; while another divifion of the
army under General *Shepard*, marched to the fame
place, by a different route.   But, before their arrival there, an adjuftment took place between the
infurgents, who had collected about two hundred
and fifty men in the town of *Lee*, in order to ftop
the courts, and the militia, who muftered to the
number of about three hundred, with a determination to protect them.   The fubftance of the a-
greement was, that the infurgents fhould difperfe,
and that the commander of the militia fhould, in
cafe they were purfued by government, ufe his
perfonal endeavours, to have them tried within
their own county.

WHEN the army arrived at *Pittsfield*, a party
were immediately detached in fleighs, under the
command

command of the Adjutant General, to the town of *Dalton*, in purfuit of *Wiley* ; and another under the command of Capt. *Francis*, on a fimilar undertaking to *Williamstown*. Both of them returned on the next day. The firft party took fix prifoners, among whom was *Wiley*'s fon ; *Wiley* himfelf having made his efcape. The other party took fourteen prifoners, after meeting with fome refiftance, in which one of their men was wounded.

WHILE the army were marching through the country, and bearing down all oppofition before them, a fpirit of uneafinefs frequently broke out in their rear. In the county of *Worcefter*, where Major General *Jonathan Warner* was in command, a number of the infurgents affembled at *Newbraintree*, making prifoners of travellers, and infulting the friends of government. Upon information of this, on the 2d of *February*, a party of about one hundred and fifty in fleighs, and twenty on horfeback, were difpatched from *Worcefter*, to difperfe them. On the approach of this force, the infurgents went fome diftance from their quarters, and fecreted themfelves behind the ftone walls : Hence they fired upon the militia, and immediately fled to the woods. Two perfons were badly wounded by their fire, but the

K   party

party purfued their courfe to a houfe, where the main body of the infurgents were fuppofed to have been lodged. Upon their arrival here however, they were greatly difappointed, in finding only a few of the enemy, who had been placed as a guard over their prifoners ; the reft having effected their efcape. They therefore proceeded to *Rutland*, and returned the next day, with four of the infurgents whom they had captured.

THE effects which the defeat of the malcontents had impreffed upon their minds, and which they wifhed to communicate to their friends, who had tarried behind, were remarkably difcovered by the following letter, which was tranfmitted into the ftate, as it is faid, by one of their leaders.

"*Berkfhire, February* 15, 1787.

" FRIENDS AND FELLOW SUFFERERS,

" WILL you now tamely fuffer your arms to be taken from you, your eftates to be confifcated, and even fwear to fupport a conftitution and form of government, and likewife a code of laws, which common fenfe and your confciences declare to be iniquitous and cruel ? And can you bear to fee and hear of the yeomanry of this Commonwealth being parched, and cut to pieces by the cruel and mercilefs tools of tyrannical power,

and

and not refent it even unto relentlefs bloodfhed ?
Would to God, I had the tongue of a ready wri-
ter, that I might imprefs on your minds the idea
of the obligation you, as citizens of a republican
government, are under to fupport thofe rights and
privileges that the God of nature hath entitled
you to. Let me now perfuade you, by all the
facred ties of friendfhip, which natural affection
infpires the human heart with, immediately to
turn out and affert your rights.

" THE firft ftep that I would recommend, is to
deftroy *Shepard*'s army, then proceed to the county of *Berkfhire*, as we are now collecting at *New-
lebanon*, in *York* ftate, and *Pownal* in *Vermont*
ftate, with a determination to carry our point, if
fire, blood and carnage will effect it : Therefore
we beg that every friend will immediately proceed to the county of *Berkfhire*, and help us to
Burgoyne *Lincoln* and his army. I beg this may
immediately circulate through your county.

" I AM, gentlemen, in behalf of myfelf and
other officers, your

" Humble fervant,
" ELI PARSONS."

ON the 16th of *February*, General *Shepard* detached a party of horfe from *Northfield*, under
K 2   the

the command of Captain *Samuel Buffington*, for the purpose of apprehending certain infurgents, who had fled to *Vermont*. Upon their arrival, within that government, although they procured a warrant from a magiftrate, to apprehend the objects of their fearch, yet the people affembled in fuch numbers, and evidenced fuch a hoftile difpofition towards them, that they were obliged to relinquifh their purfuit, and return to *Maffachufetts*. They however, in the evening, fent a fmall number from their body, among whom was Mr. *Jacob Walker*, to fecure one *Jafon Parmenter*, who had acted as a Captain with the infurgents. Unfortunately for *Walker*, they foon overtook the perfon whom they were fent after, accompanied in his flight by feveral others. The fleighs of the oppofite parties, unexpectedly run upon each other ; and, on *Parmenter*'s hailing, and receiving no anfwer, he ordered his men to fire ; but mifchief was prevented, by their guns not going off. *Parmenter* and *Walker* then raifed their pieces together and fired. The latter was fhot through the body, and died in half an hour. The furvivor and his affociates, efcaped by the help of the woods and a deep fnow, into *Vermont*, where however, they were all taken the next day, by a body of infantry, detached from the militia by Captain *Buffington* :

And

And *Parmenter* was afterwards tried, and convicted of treason.

THE period for which the militia were detached, having expired on the twenty firft of *February,* and the troops under the new inliftment, not having arrived in any great numbers, the rebels determined to embrace fo favourable an opportunity of making an incurfion into the ftate, as well for the purpofe of plunder, as of taking feveral refpectable characters, and among others, General *Lincoln* himfelf. Their profpect upon this occafion was fuch, as might have almoft infured fuccefs, had their motions been properly timed : For, in the exchanging of the militia, the General was once left with only about thirty men. But, from mifinformation, or fome other caufe, this moment, fo aufpicious to their views, was neglected. On the 26th of the month however, a large body of them under a Capt. *Hamlin,* entered the county of *Berkfhire,* from the ftate of *Newyork,* and proceeded to the town of *Stockbridge.* This they pillaged at pleafure, and made prifoners of a great number of the moft reputable inhabitants. The militia of *Sheffield* were collected upon the firft information of this event, and were joined by thofe of *Greatbarrington* about one o'clock on the 27th. The whole, making eighty, were com-

K 3 manded

manded by Col. *John Afbley*, jun. and after
marching in feveral directions, to meet the enemy, they finally returned to *Sheffield*, and came up
with them there. The fevereft engagement took
place at this time, that happened during the conteft. The rebels began a fcattering fire at a diftance ; whereupon the militia advanced rapidly
towards them, and the action became general. It
was warmly fupported by both fides, for the fpace
of about fix minutes, during which time many of
the government's troops difcharged that number
of rounds. The rebels then gave way, and fled
in various directions. They left two dead near
the place of action, and upwards of thirty of
them were wounded, among whom was *Hamlin*, their Captain. Another party of militia
arriving immediately after the fkirmifh, enabled the conquerors to take more than fifty of
the enemy prifoners. The lofs on the fide of
the militia, confifted of only two men killed
and one wounded. Of the former, one was a
prifoner with the rebels before the action, and
probably met with his fate from the fire of his
friends, by a barbarous practice which his captors
adopted, of putting their prifoners in the front, as
well to check the ardour of the militia, from a
fenfe of their danger, as to fcreen themfelves.
But in addition to this lofs, ought to be reckoned,

ed, that of two amiable young men and intimate friends, whose habits of body were unequal to enduring the fatigue of the rapid march which this party performed, and who, after languishing under the effects of their exertions, died with peculiar marks of sympathetick grief for each other.

THE lodgment which the rebels effected in the neighbouring states, after their expulsion from *Petersham,* besides exposing the Commonwealth to a predatory war, which no force could prevent, was attended with another very serious evil. By their communication with the inhabitants, they diffused their principles, and created a partiality for their cause, which was said, in one state, to have reached the government itself. An inattention to authority, and a lurking disposition to enforce popular plans by insurrections, had appeared in several parts of the continent, and there was great room to fear, that a less operative cause than the emigration of so many incendiaries, might light up this passion, and throw the whole union into a flame. Aware of this, as well as of the impossibility of conquering a party who could, at any time, secure a retreat in other territories, the General Court early requested the Governour, to write to the Governours of the neighbouring states, to offer a reward for apprehending the reb-

els,

els, and to take meafures for preventing their receiving any fupplies. But, from one caufe and another, though his Excellency's letters were repeatedly fent to urge this fubject, effectual meafures were not fo readily adopted by all the ftates adjoining, as the legiflature feemed to expect.

THE anfwer from the Governour of *Rhodeifland*, on the 15th of *February*, was indeed the firft, in point of time, though it can hardly be called fo, in refpect to the profpect which it held up, of efficacious meafures being adopted by that ftate, for fuppreffing the rebellion. However, after fome general obfervations, upon the difficulty of curing evils in the body politick, he concluded, that he would ftrictly adhere to the Governour's requeft, and do every thing in his power to cooperate with him, in fupporting peace, order and good government. But the authority of *Rhodeifland* was far from taking fteps to fecure the fugitives from juftice, who publickly reforted there. When a motion was made in their affembly, (upon the act of *Maffachufetts* for apprehending the principals of the rebellion being read) that a law fhould be paffed, requefting their Governour to iffue a proclamation alfo for apprehending them, if within that ftate, it was loft by a great majority ; And one of the very refugees was allowed a feat within their chamber.

THE

THE Governour of *Connecticut,* in his anfwer of the 20th of the fame month, was much more direct and decifive in his affurances of affiftance. He informed the Governour of the Commonwealth, that if the rebels fhould feek an afylum in *Connecticut,* they would be immediately apprehended, and delivered up ; and, in cafe of their reaffembling, they would be effectually prevented from receiving fupplies, as the inhabitants of his government viewed the rebels with a ftrong degree of averfion. In addition to this, he iffued a proclamation, offering a reward for apprehending the rebel leaders, as requefted by the Governour of *Maffachufetts* ; and, in the month of *May* following, the affembly of *Connecticut,* upon information that certain perfons were attempting to excite their inhabitants to join the infurgents, paffed a refolution for apprehending them, and even calling out the militia, if neceffary, to prevent the execution of their evil purpofes. This meafure was attended with fuccefs, as the incendiaries were, in fact, apprehended and confined.

THE government of *Newhampfhire,* where the legiflature were not fitting, purfued every meafure, which it was thought the powers vefted in the Prefident and Council would authorize. They did not think proper, to admit armed parties

ties from another state to enter that; but the existing laws permitted civil officers of other states, to pursue offenders there, and, by application to a magistrate, to have them apprehended and sent into the state having jurisdiction of the offence. They therefore directed a Major General, to secure all armed parties who might come into their state; and a proclamation was issued by their President, agreeably to the request of the Governour of the Commonwealth.

NO answers having been received from the Governours of *Newyork* or *Vermont*, the General Court, after the incursion into *Stockbridge*, requested the Governour, on the 8th of *March*, to write again to the Governour of *Newyork* by express, urging him in pressing terms, that effectual measures might be taken for apprehending such of the rebels as had fled and taken refuge there, and removing them to *Massachusetts*, agreeably to the articles of confederation, which declared, that the *United States* thereby entered into a firm league of friendship with each other, for their common defence, the security of their liberties, and their mutual and general welfare; binding themselves to assist each other against all force offered to, or attacks made upon them, or any of them, on account of religion, sovereignty, trade,

or

or any other pretence whatever. And, that if any person guilty of, or chargeable with treason, felony, or high misdemeanour in any state, should flee from justice, and be found in any of the *United States*, he should, upon demand of the Governour, or executive power of the state from which he fled, be delivered up, and removed to the state having jurisdiction of the offence. And further requesting, that the Governour of *Newyork* would permit the forces of the Commonwealth to march within the limits of his jurisdiction, when necessary; and that all officers and citizens of that state might be directed to afford them aid, and prohibited assisting the rebels.

BUT before these proceedings respecting the government of *Newyork* took place, measures had been pursued from another quarter, though unknown to the General Court, for effecting the same object. After the engagement at *Sheffield*, General *Lincoln* dispatched an express to the Governour of that state, representing the continuance and support of the rebels within one district of it, and giving information of the incursion which took place on the 26th. Upon this communication being laid before their legislature, they resolved to recommend it to the Governour, to repair as soon as possible to the place where the in-

furgents

furgents fhould be, and to call out fuch military
force from the militia of *Newyork*, and to take
command of any militia that might arrive from
Maffachufetts, and purfue all other legal meafures
he might deem neceffary, for apprehending fuch
of the infurgents as might be found within their
ftate, and for preferving the peace againft their
defigns. And they further fignified their confent
to the Governour's abfenting himfelf from the
ftate, from time to time, as exigencies might require. Immediately upon this refolution being
paffed, the Governour proceeded to execute the
defign therein expreffed. General Orders were
iffued, by which a brigade and three regiments
of the militia, were directed to hold themfelves
in readinefs to march at a moment's warning, and
reafons drawn from conftitutional and federal
principles, were urged with propriety and force,
to induce a prompt obedience in the militia, to
his commands. After an interview with General
Lincoln, he went on, accompanied by that commander, to *Newconcord*, where a number of his
officers were affembled to meet him. Thofe of the
civil department were directed to call on the militia of *Newyork*, or on the military officers of
Maffachufetts, for fuch force as might be neceffary, in apprehending or difperfing the infurgents.
Thefe decifive meafures obliged the malcontents

to

to flee out of the ftate of *Newyork*, and to betake themfelves to their laft 'refort in *Vermont*.

WITH refpect to that government, the legiflature had been officially informed, That on the 13th of *February*, General *Lincoln* difpatched *Royal Tyler*, Efq; one of his Aids de Camp, to requeft their affiftance in apprehending the rebel ringleaders : That, upon his communicating his inftructions and requeft in writing, the fubject of them was put in committee, and a report made for requeft-ing their Governour to iffue his proclamation, enjoining it upon their citizens, not to harbour the leaders or abettors of the rebels : That this report was accepted by their lower Houfe, and fent up to their Council, where there alfo appear-ed eight of nine affiftants in favour of it : That it would of courfe, have paffed there, but for the Governour's objections, which were at firft found-ed upon his not having given the fubject a proper confideration, but were afterwards bottomed up-on more ferious principles :—Thefe were faid to have been raifed, from the impolicy of iffuing a proclamation, which might impede the emigra-tion of fubjects from other ftates into that ; and the imprudence of oppofing the fenfe of their peo-ple, who began to affemble in arms, in a neigh-bouring town, and who might create an infur-

reftion,

rection, and surround the legiflature, unlefs the report were difmiffed : That there being no profpect of Mr. *Tyler*'s effecting the object of his requeft, and the letters from the Governour of *Maffachufetts* having arrived, he departed, with ftrong apprehenfions, that the bulk of the people in *Vermont*, were for affording protection to the rebels, and that no immediate or effectual aid would be granted, in confequence of either. The General Court therefore, on the fame day, requefted the Governour to write again to the Governour of that ftate alfo, reprefenting the religious and political obligations neighbouring ftates were under, to prevent fugitives from juftice harbouring themfelves within their refpective territories ; reminding the government of *Vermont* of the liberal principles on which *Maffachufetts* had conducted towards them, and of her unwillingnefs to entertain a doubt of a different conduct on their part ; informing them of the general notoriety, that a number of the leaders, and others concerned in the rebellion, had taken fhelter, and received fuccour among their citizens, whereby not only the inhabitants of *Maffachufetts*, but the government of *Vermont*, was in danger ; that this had been reprefented to them in a friendly letter from his Excellency, and although no anfwer was received, yet that the Court conceived, that they

had

had a right to expect a ready and full compliance with the request therein expressed. And further requesting the Governour of *Vermont*, to deliver up the rebels who had taken refuge within his limits, or to permit the forces of *Massachusetts* to enter those limits, for the purpose of apprehending them, and to direct all officers of *Vermont*, to aid them in that purpose.

PREVIOUSLY however to the passing of this spirited resolution, the Governour of *Vermont* issued his proclamation of the 27th of *February*, and afterwards communicated the same to the Governour of *Massachusetts*, in a letter, containing friendly assurances of cooperation in measures, for effectually checking so daring and dangerous an evil, as the intestine faction which then prevailed.

THE legislature of *Pennsylvania*, the President of which state was also included in the Governour's letters, shewed a generous compliance with his Excellency's request. On the 1st of *March* they made an addition to the reward offered by *Massachusetts*, for apprehending the leaders of the rebellion, if taken within their state. Their resolution was communicated by their President, in a congratulatory letter upon the success of the measures adopted for preserving a constitution,

which

which he was pleafed to denominate one of the beft in the union, if not in the world.

THE General Court alfo empowered the Governour, on the 8th of *March*, in conformity with the conftitution, to march the militia raifed for fubduing the rebellion out of the limits of the commonwealth, into the bounds of any of the ftates adjacent, if he fhould think it neceffary for that purpofe. In addition to a former requeft to the Governour, to write to Congrefs, to inform them that a rebellion exifted in the Commonwealth, and to requeft that they would take meafures for defending the arfenal at *Springfield*, in order that the troops there might be employed in other fervice ; they further defired his Excellency, to requeft of Congrefs, that the federal troops raifed in *Newyork* and the ftates eaftward of it, might be directed, to afford their aid, in apprehending, and, if neceffary, in deftroying the rebels, in any place within the limits of the *United States*. And that Congrefs would give to General *Lincoln* a commiffion, under the authority of the *United States*, to march the forces of *Maffachufetts* into any territory, within the ftates, for the purpofe of apprehending their leaders, and bringing them to juftice.

AS

As soon as the insurgents were subdued within the state, and measures taken for precluding them a toleration in the neighbouring governments, the General Court found it a suitable time for providing for the trials of such as were in custody. For this purpose, on the 26th of *February*, the Supreme Judicial Court were directed, by law, to hold a special session in the disaffected counties of *Berkshire*, *Hampshire* and *Middlesex*, the standing laws providing for their sitting in *Worcester* on the last Tuesday in *April*. And in order that the trials should be made by disinterested and unprejudiced juries, a law was also passed, reciting, that whereas the pardon to the rebels was granted on condition, that the persons concerned should not serve as jurors for three years; and whereas it was reasonable to provide, as far as might be, not only for the due administration of justice, but also for the relief of such persons as had been concerned in the rebellion, and who, though unwilling to declare themselves criminal, might wish to avail themselves of the pardon which was, or might be promised: Therefore it was enacted, that the selectmen of the several towns, to which venires should be issued for jurors within one year, should withdraw from the jury boxes the names of all such persons as they might judge had been guilty of favouring the re-

L   bellion,

bellion, or of giving aid or fupport thereto, prior
to their drawing out the names of the jurors that
might be called for by the venires. Provided
however, that if fuch perfons fhould make application to the town to reftore their names to
the jury box, and could obtain a vote of the
town, at any town meeting afterwards to be called
for that purpofe, to have their names fo reftored
again, the names of fuch perfons fhould be reftored accordingly. This law further enacted,
that for the purpofe of preventing thofe perfons
who had been concerned in the rebellion, from
ferving as jurors in trials for treafon or mifprifion
of treafon, in cafe the attorney for the Commonwealth, in the trial of any perfon for the afore-
named crimes, fhould fuggeft to the court, that
any perfons called to ferve on the jury of trials
had been guilty of favouring the rebellion, or had
been in any manner concerned therein, or given
aid or fupport thereto, if the court, upon inquiry
of the perfon againft whom the fuggeftion fhould
be made, or upon examination of witneffes, fhould
judge that there was probable ground for the fuggeftion, it fhould be the duty of the court to fet
afide the perfon fo objected to, as difqualified to
ferve as a juror, in the fame manner as had before
been practifed, in cafe a juror felt himfelf preju-
diced in any caufe.

BUT,

BUT, the extent of the rebellion had been too general, to allow of the indiscriminate operation of law. Such had been its prevalence in some towns, that when the disqualifying act came into force, it scarcely left sufficient numbers for the necessary offices of the corporation. It therefore, became equally an act of humanity and good policy, to invent some method for screening from the laws, many who yet remained, among such multitudes, obnoxious to the severest penalties. With this view the General Court, on the 10th of *March*, appointed three commissioners, whose duty it was, upon application made to them, by or in behalf of any persons concerned in the rebellion, and not included in the act of indemnity, after due inquiry into their character and conduct, to promise indemnity to them, on their taking and subscribing the oath of allegiance to the Commonwealth, provided satisfactory evidence should be produced in their favour, that they were duly penitent for their crimes, and properly disposed to return to their allegiance, and discharge the duty of faithful citizens. And this indemnity was, at the discretion of the commissioners, to be promised with or without any or all of the conditions, &c. enumerated in the act aforementioned ; and with or without the farther condition of the offender's being bound to keep

the

the peace, and to be of good behaviour for a term not exceeding three years.

THE powers of the commissioners were likewise extended, to make remission of the conditions of the disqualifying act, in whole or in part, to those who were entitled to the benefits of it. Provided that their attention to those persons, should not interfere with the duty first assigned them.

FROM the protection of this commission however, were excluded four of the rebel leaders, *Shays*, *Wheeler*, *Parsons*, and *Luke Day*, together with all persons who had fired upon, or killed any of the citizens in the peace of the Commonwealth, and the commander of the party to which such persons belonged. Also the members of the rebel council of war, and all persons against whom the Governour and Council had issued a warrant, unless liberated on bail.

IN order to derive every advantage from the execution of this important commission, very respectable and honourable characters were appointed for that purpose. These consisted of the Hon. *Benjamin Lincoln*, Esq; the Commander of the Army ; the Hon. *Samuel Phillips*, jun. Esq; the President of the Senate; and the Hon. *Samuel Allyne Otis*, Esq; Speaker of the late House of Representatives.

FROM

FROM thefe meafures it was hoped, that the benefits of pardon would at length be forced, as it were, upon many infatuated citizens, whofe obftinacy had repeatedly led them to reject offers of mercy with fcorn ; while the difpatch with which the neceffary examples of juftice would be made, would fhew their punifhment to be the immediate and juft confequence of their crimes.

WHILE the General Court were making this liberal provifion for reftoring the rebels to their privileges, they thought it neceffary to provide fome check againft feigned converts being fuddenly admitted into places of truft. They therefore paffed a refolution, directing that felectmen and other town officers, fhould take and fubfcribe the oath of allegiance to the Commonwealth.

NOTWITHSTANDING the attention neceffary to be paid to the fuppreffing of the rebellion, and the defence of the ftate, the General Court did not lofe fight of the fyftem of reform begun at their laft feffion. They paffed the bill for reducing the number of terms of holding the Courts of Common Pleas and General Seffions of the Peace, in the feveral counties ; and they enacted a new fee bill, by which the allowances made to publick officers were confiderably leffened. They alfo appointed a committee to inquire, whether

L 3

there

there were any real publick grievances under which the people of the Commonwealth laboured. This committee reported but three, which were the following :

" 1ſt. That ſuitable proviſion had not been made, for the ſeaſonable and punƈtual payment of the intereſt due on publick ſecurities.

" 2d. That the Treaſurer had not been laid under greater reſtriƈtions, with regard to the draw-ing of orders. And,

" 3d. That the ſalary eſtabliſhed by law for the ſupport of the firſt magiſtrate of the Common-wealth, was higher than was reaſonable."

THE laſt article in this report did not fail to at-traƈt the attention of the legiſlature. A long de-bate enſued upon the ſubjeƈt of it, and the reſult was, that the two houſes paſſed a bill for reduc-ing the Governour's ſalary the enſuing year, from 1100l. to 800l. This bill his Excellency returned, with his objeƈtions, founded upon that article of the conſtitution which provides,

" THAT as the publick good requires that the Governour ſhould not be under the undue influence of any of the members of the General Court, by a dependence on them for his ſupport; that he ſhould, in all caſes, aƈt with freedom for the benefit of the publick ; that he ſhould not have his atten-

tion

tion neceſſarily diverted from that object to his private concerns ; and that he ſhould maintain the dignity of the Commonwealth, in the character of its chief magiſtrate ; it is neceſſary that he ſhould have an honourable, ſtated ſalary, and of a fixed and permanent value, amply ſufficient for thoſe purpoſes, and eſtabliſhed by ſtanding laws : And it ſhall be among the firſt acts of the General Court, after the commencement of this conſtitution, to eſtabliſh ſuch ſalary by law accordingly.

" PERMANENT and honourable ſalaries ſhall alſo be eſtabliſhed by law, for the juſtices of the Supreme Judicial Court.

" AND if it ſhall be found, that any of the ſalaries aforeſaid, ſo eſtabliſhed, are inſufficient, they ſhall from time to time be enlarged as the General Court ſhall judge proper."

UPON this occaſion the Governour by a written meſſage aſked, Whether, by this article, the right of ſettling the quantum of the ſalary, was not confined to the firſt General Court, after the commencement of the conſtitution ? Whether any power was given to any ſucceeding General Court, to alter that quantum, unleſs it ſhould be inſufficient ; in which caſe, it might be enlarged as the

court

court fhould judge proper? Whether, if it were alterable by diminution, by the then General Court, it might not, in the fame manner, be altered by the next General Court; and again further altered by fucceeding General Courts; and thus, inftead of being eftablifhed, whether it would be any thing more than an annual grant, conftantly fubject to variation and change? Whether, in that cafe, it could be deemed a ftated falary; or of a fixed and permanent value; or eftablifhed by any ftanding or permanent law; or could be depended on as amply fufficient for the purpofes intended? And whether thofe purpofes as expreffed in the conftitution, would in that cafe be anfwered?

THE Governour difavowed any interefted motives influencing him to make thefe objections, declaring that fhould there be a future opportunity for it, and the General Court fhould then think the propofed reduction worthy of their notice, he would, fo far as it might refpect himfelf, confent to it, although his annual expenditures did much exceed the whole amount of his falary. But, that it was not in his power, for the reafons ftated, nor did it comport with his inclination to diminifh, or in any way render precarious, the falary of his fucceffours.

THESE

THESE objections were of such force, that thirty
fix only, out of fixty five members in the lower
Houfe, were in favour of paffing the bill, after
they were made : So that it was in fact negatived ;
the conftitution requiring two thirds of the members prefent in both Houfes, to give efficacy to a
meafure under fuch circumftances.

ON the fame day, *March* 10th, the Governour,
at the requeft of the two Houfes, put an end to the
third feffion of the General Court and, as it was
then fuppofed, to their further agency in the affairs
of the Commonwealth, by a prorogation to the
next annual election. In taking our leave of this
memorable feffion, we fhall be indulged in ob-
ferving, that the acts of the legiflature were directed at an object entirely new, and of courfe, were
unaffifted by precedent. No rebellion had heretofore marked the annals of *Maffachufetts*, either
under the royal or republican government. Upon the hiftories of European nations, a reliance
could be placed fo far only as the genius and circumftances of the people of the two hemifpheres
agreed. But who could fay, that principles and
meafures which might perfuade or terrify the
mind of the mountaineer of *Scotland* or *Wales*,
would have the fame effect upon the unconquer-
ed fpirit of the weftern inhabitants of *Maffachu-*
fetts ?

fetts ? No lefs difficulty arofe from the divifions in the fentiments of the citizens. To afcertain the courfe which the publick mind would take, required a forefight little fhort of prophecy. Whether that thirft for freedom which the people had difcovered in the late revolution, would, from miftaken principles, decline to an unqualified oppofition to authority, or whether it would rife into a difdainful refentment againft the enemies of juft laws, who are always the real enemies of liberty, feemed to be referved for futurity alone to determine. The conftitution alfo was recent in its ftanding, and unfettled by practice. To enforce it in that point, where the powers of government begin to encroach upon the moft favourite rights of the fubject, was to encounter not only the clamours of the difcontented, but the jealoufy of the whole people.

UNDER fuch circumftances, to mark the exact point at which force ought to begin, or the exact degree to which it ought to extend, exceeded perhaps, the calculation of the legiflature. But if vigorous meafures were delayed too long, it was an errour which arofe from too great a confidence in the operation of reafon and reflection upon the minds of the infurgents, and from the tardinefs with which the publick fentiment feemed

ed at firſt to recede from their cauſe. If the penalties
inflicted upon the culprits were ſevere, it is a ſufficient apology, if not a juſtification, that they
were not inflicted until the free, unſolicited pardon of government had been twice tendered to
them, and rejected with contempt; nor, until they
had made their appeal to arms, with evident deſigns, and no ſmall expectations of conquering
the government, and overturning the conſtitution.
In ſhort, the proviſion which was made at the laſt
ſtage of the penal ſyſtem, for checking its operation almoſt univerſally, when the ends of it ſhould
be effected by the voluntary acts of the offenders,
muſt forever acquit the government, in the minds
of every impartial judge, from any ſanguinary or
revengeful deſign.

IN the receſs of the legiſlature, the commiſſion-
ers for granting indemnity to perſons concerned
in the rebellion, were employed in the mild exer-
ciſe of their authority; whilſt the Supreme Judicial Court were proceeding in the no leſs neceſſary, though leſs thankful office, of trying the offenders. Seven hundred and ninety perſons took
the benefit of the commiſſion. Of thoſe who
were tried at this circuit, there were ſix convicted
of treaſon in the county of *Berkſhire*, the ſame
number in *Hampſhire*, one in *Worceſter*, and one
afterwards

afterwards in *Middlesex* ; all of whom received sentence of death. Besides these, there were also large numbers convicted of seditious words and practices ; many of whom were persons of consequence, and some of them in office. Among others, a member of the House of Representatives, after being apprehended by a state warrant, was convicted of these offences, and sentenced to the ignominious punishment of sitting on the gallows with a rope about his neck, paying a fine of 50 l. and being bound to keep the peace, and to be of good behaviour, for five years ; and this sentence was accordingly put in execution.

THE same inclination to mercy, which had induced the legislature to make frequent acts of indemnity, was visible in the conduct of the executive branch of government. Out of the number of convicts in the western counties, who had forfeited their lives to justice, the council advised, that two only should suffer death in *Berkshire*, and as many in *Hampshire*. To the remaining eight, the Governour extended a free pardon on the 30th of *April* ; and, on the 17th of *May*, a reprieve was granted to their less fortunate companions, to the 21st of *June* following.

THE

THE death of the Treasurer afforded an unexpected occasion, for calling the legislature together the fourth time in the present year. Upon their assembling on the 27th day of *April*, the Governour took that opportunity, after the necessary communications of business, to express his wish for retirement, and (alluding to the turn which the votes for the chief magistrate had taken) his happiness, that the voice of the people coincided with it, as he could not otherwise have indulged it, without the imputation of deserting them in the critical situation of their affairs. His Excellency took his leave of the Court, and conferred his best wishes on the Commonwealth; among other things, that the people might have just ideas of liberty, and not lose it in licentiousness, and in despotism its natural consequence.

NOTHING material to the rebellion appeared in the proceedings of the Court, during this session, which continued but nine days, excepting a report of the commissioners appointed to grant pardons to the offenders. The most operative causes to which they assigned the late disturbances, were publick and private debts, which arose principally from an undue use of articles of foreign growth and manufacture; and a delusion with respect to the proceedings of the General Court, and the
situation

fituation of things in the different parts of the Commonwealth. They alfo obferved, that they were obliged in duty to declare, although it was painful to make the declaration, that from the reprefentations which had been made, there was great reafon to believe that too many perfons, who had been members of the General Court, inftead of giving that information of the reafons and principles, upon which the acts and refolves of the legiflature had been founded, which might have fatisfied the rational enquirer, and have filenced the unreafonable complainer, had by their converfation and conduct, irritated and inflamed the reftlefs and uneafy, and alarmed the peaceable uninformed citizen.

UPON their rifing, the court anfwered the Governour's addrefs. In this, they accorded with him in his fatisfaction, on the fuccefs of the meafures which had been adopted, for fubduing the rebellion. They declared that their confidence in his Excellency's character, was the dictate of real fentiment ; and, expreffing the hopes which might be entertained from his abilities and virtues, they plainly diffented from the wifh which he entertained for retirement : Adding their own defire, that he might receive thofe marks of efteem and benevolent affection, from a grateful people, which are the proper reward of diftinguifhed merit.

THE

THE heart of the rebellion being broken, by the return of many of its abettors to their allegiance, and the exclusion of the rest from the state, the views of the malcontents became confined chiefly to the securing of their leaders, and of those who were under sentence of death. They had left no expedient untried, to render themselves formidable upon a larger plan. Several of their leaders had proceeded to the province of *Canada*, to solicit succours from that government; but this adventure was not attended with success. Their predatory incursions had been represented as preludes to a general invasion, and magnified with ostentatious and malignant threats. Their weakness however, was too evident to admit of their extending their object beyond what we have mentioned : But this they pretended to have some expectation of effecting, from the pardon and reprieve which had been granted to the convicts ; a circumstance which they affected to construe into a fear, on the part of the government, to execute the sentence of the judicial department.

THE hostilities of the field were succeeded by less destructive, though not less determined contests, at the elections. Every party resorted to this source, for constitutional means of effecting their wishes. Those who were for preserving the
dignity

dignity of government ; thofe who hoped to mel-
iorate the exifting fyftem againft the rebels, and
thofe who were too much wearied with war, and
too little attached to either fide, to look after any
other objects than the immediate quiet of the
Commonwealth, by whatever means it might be
effected, all applied themfelves to the elections.
When the bufinefs was over, fuch alterations were
made in the reprefentations of towns ; fuch divifions appeared in the votes for Senators ; and the
change in the chair was effected by fo large a
majority, as feemed to indicate a revolution in
the publick mind.

UPON the meeting of the new General Court
therefore, the curiofity and anxiety of the inhabitants were not lefs raifed, than when the con-
troverfy was doubtful in the field. The infurgents had always requefted, that the decifion of
their caufe might be referred to a new affembly.
They fpoke of them with confidence, as a body
who would demonftrate, upon the juft principles
of reprefentation, that they were the majority of
the people. When the returns of the Reprefentatives were publifhed, it was in fact found,
whatever might be the fentiments of the members,
that about a quarter of them only had been in the
late Houfe. Several perfons, who in the war

had

had been thrown into prifon as dangerous to the Commonwealth, who had fled from ftate warrants into neighbouring governments, or who had prefided in county conventions, and otherwife manifefted their oppofition to the late ruling authority, were now to be feen on the feats of the legiflature. Such a reverfe of things drew the eyes of all upon the new Court, who were viewed with emotions of expectation and concern.

THE conteft being thus, in a great meafure, removed from the military department, and carried into the legiflature, where it may be faid to have begun, the firft fubject which offered for trying the ftrength of parties, was the filling up of the vacancies in the Senate, and the elections of Counfellors. To guard the Senate againft paper money and a tender act, and to give vigour to the Council, was the object of one fide. To introduce a fpirit of clemency and pardon into the Council, on whofe vote the lives of convicted rebels were fufpended, and to incline the Senate to popular reforms, was the object of the other. In this ftruggle, though it may not affift us in deciding which party prevailed, yet it is a circumftance worthy of notice, as expreffive of the thirft for novelty, which reigned at this time, that the Council underwent nearly the fame changes as the lower houfe; two thirds of their

M   number

number confifting of perfons who had never offi-
ciated in that ftation before.

THE great queftion of means for the final fup-
preffion of the rebellion, did not long keep out of
fight; and the infurgents themfelves once more
furnifhed an incident, for affecting the minds of
the members with unfavourable impreffions to
their caufe. In one of their incurfions, which
happened on the 21ft of *May*, as Mr. *Jofeph Met-
calf* was returning home, upon a journey, they
made him their prifoner; and, on the night following, they attacked the houfe of *Medad Pomeroy*, Efq; in *Warwick*, and captured him alfo.
Both thefe gentlemen, who fupported very refpectable characters, and who were generally
known in the country, were conveyed to places
without the ftate. A paper was left at the houfe
of Mr. *Pomeroy*, purporting that the perfons tak-
en were to be referved as hoftages, to fecure the
lives of *Jafon Parmenter* and *Henry M'Culloch*,
who were under fentence of death for high treafon; and that, if thefe fhould be put to death by
the ftate, the perfons then captured, would be put
to death alfo, without delay. Such a high hand-
ed fyftem of retaliation, was truly inconfiftent
with the debilitated ftate of the rebel forces, and
with a retreat which they held by the courtfey, and
precarious indulgence of a neighbouring ftate.
This

This indeed was soon evinced by the escape of their prisoners, not as was supposed without their own connivance.

WHATEVER expectations the malcontents might have entertained, from the great change in the elections, the language of the chair, in which Governour *Hancock* was this year replaced, was manly and decisive, upon communicating the intelligence of these incursions. His Excellency submitted it to the consideration of the Court, whether it would not be absolutely necessary for the support and protection of government, to continue in service the troops then stationed in the counties of *Hampshire* and *Berkshire*, for so long a time, after the term of their inlistment should expire, as they might judge necessary, to restore peace, tranquillity and security to those counties.

THE committee on this message, reported a resolution for requesting the Governour to raise eight hundred men, to be stationed in the western counties for six months, unless sooner discharged. To this resolution the Senate assented, but after it had been once debated in the House, they sent down an order, in connexion with it, for raising a committee to consider the expediency of repealing the disqualifying act, and of reporting a bill of indemnity, under certain restrictions and excep-

M 2

tions

tions to such persons connected in the rebellion, as would take the oath of allegiance to the Commonwealth within a certain time; and in general, to consider the most effectual measures for restoring peace and tranquillity to the Commonwealth. In the debates upon a concurrence with the Senate in this order, the sense and feelings of the House began to be discoverable. An attempt was made to direct the indemnity to be indiscriminate, without any restrictions or exceptions; but it was not supported by one quarter part of the House, which at that time consisted of two hundred members. It was however, at length, agreed that the committee should be permitted to report the bill with restrictions and exceptions, or otherwise: And in this the Senate concurred.

ALTHOUGH it was foreseen, that the report of this committee would be intimately connected with the resolution of the Senate, or perhaps entirely supersede it; and although one great objection to it was, that another pardon did not accompany it, yet the House would not postpone the consideration of the resolution, till the report was made, but debated upon it until the Senate sent for it, and substituted the report in its place.

DURING these debates, the House, for the ease of some members of the western counties, who

were

were extremely diſſatisfied at the delay of the buſineſs, unanimouſly reſolved, That the end of the
ſocial compact was to ſecure the exiſtence of the
body politick, and to furniſh the individuals who
compoſe it, with the power of enjoying in ſafety
and tranquillity their natural rights, and the
bleſſings of life; and that, therefore, the Houſe
conſidered it as their firſt, greateſt, and moſt eſ-
ſential duty, not only to take the moſt effectual
methods to eſtabliſh and confirm them; but that
they would employ all the powers veſted in them
by the conſtitution, civil and military, to give per-
manency and effect to theſe important objects.

THE report of the laſt committee conſiſted of a
reſolution for raiſing a number of men, not exceeding eight hundred, nor leſs than five hundred,
to be ſtationed in the weſtern counties; and for
pardoning all perſons concerned in the rebellion,
upon their taking and ſubſcribing the oath of allegiance on or before the 12th day of *September*
following, excepting eight, to whom the Senate
added a ninth.

IN debating the report by paragraphs, the favourite meaſure of introducing a general pardon
was again, for the laſt time, attempted, but without ſucceſs, as out of two hundred fourteen members, ninety four only were in favour of it. The
ſame fate attended various motions for leſſening

M 3   the

the number of the excepted perfons ; and on the queftion of concurrence with the Senate, in accepting the report, the long difputed fuperiority fell to the advocates for the meafure, by a majority of eight. The legiflative opinion was thus at length decided, refpecting the means of fuppreffing the rebellion, a fubject which had drawn fpeculations and conjectures from every quarter of the community.

NOTWITHSTANDING this important determination for the fupport of coercive meafures, fimilar to thofe of the late government, the proceedings under that authority were held up as difguftful to the prefent Houfe ; and a committee was raifed on the 14th of *June*, to bring in a bill to repeal the law for fufpending the privilege of the writ of *Habeas corpus*, and the claufe of the law requiring town officers to take and fubfcribe the oath of allegiance ; although the former of thefe laws was to expire on a day fo near, the firft of *July* following, as to admit of little more than time, for the neceffary ceremonies of enacting the bill propofed. This propofition, however, fell through from obvious reafons, and was afterwards openly renounced by its advocates.

ON the 29th of *June*, in confequence of a meffage from the Governour, his Excellency was requefted

quefted to make known to the ftates, who had a-
dopted meafures for aiding the exertions of government to fupprefs the rebellion, the juft fenfe
which the legiflature entertained of their friendly
difpofition ; and to requeft permiffion of thofe,
with whom any of the rebels had taken refuge, to
march the troops of *Maffachufetts* into their limits, for the purpofe of deftroying and conquering
them. And the Governour was empowered to
raife or detach fuch force, as might appear to him
to be neceffary for that purpofe, and to march
them out of the ftate accordingly. The legiflature alfo declared it as their determination,
that no further acts of grace and clemency could
be made, to any perfons who might be in arms a-
gainft the government, confiftently with the dignity thereof, and with that fafety and protection,
which ought to be extended to the peaceable and
well affected citizens of the Commonwealth.

THE refolution for pardoning perfons concerned in the rebellion, being found to extend only
to the crime of treafon, another was introduced
to include feditious practices. But one fide of
the Court contended, that the cofts of profecution which had arifen, fhould be paid by the
Commonwealth, while the other thought it but a
reafonable condition of the pardon, that they
fhould be paid by the culprits. Having been

M 4 much

much divided upon this point, they finally agreed upon a refolution, in general terms, that until the end of their next feffion, no profecution fhould be commenced or proceeded on, for fedition or feditious practices.

THE eye of the General Court was ftill fixed upon reforms, and a reduction of the Governour's falary, began again to be agitated. But his Excellency effectually checked all further debates upon the fubject, by a meffage, in which he voluntarily offered 300 l. of his falary for the prefent year, to the community ; fuggefting at the fame time, that when the future fituation of affairs fhould be lefs perplexed, he hoped it would not be confidered as a precedent to affect any fucceffour in office ; nor be viewed in any other light, than that of contributing, as far as in him lay, to relieve the burdens of the people.

TO this meffage both Houfes returned their thanks ; applauded the patriotifm and generofity of his Excellency ; and accepted the proffered donation. They added, that they wifhed it not to operate as a precedent to influence any fucceffour in office ; but that the conftitutionality of the queftion of leffening the falary, which the Governour had afferted to be uncertain, would without doubt, claim the attention of the legiflature when they fhould think expedient.

THE

THE ufual conditions of coercive meafures for fuppreffing the rebellion, were complied with. The tender act was continued, and a committee was raifed to confider of a more convenient place for holding the feffions of the General Court. A motion was alfo made for appointing a committee to confider the expediency of iffuing paper money; but this was loft, by the opinion of one hundred and three members out of one hundred and fifty.

THE fupplies for the troops being granted, though not without oppofition, the feffion of the General Court was finifhed on the 7th of *July*. Their meafures, though effected with lefs unanimity, were by no means fo different from thofe of their predeceffors, as appearances feemed to predict. They raifed forces, granted fupplies, indemnified offenders, and redreffed grievances much in the fame manner, as had been done for two feffions before. This uniformity of fyftem, tended greatly to annihilate the expectations of the malcontents, who prefumed that a change of men would have produced a more adequate change of meafures, with refpect to their affairs.

THE legiflature having thus provided the neceffary means for finally extinguifhing the rebellion, the publick caufe of courfe, devolved to the Supreme Executive, whofe duty it became to put thofe means into exercife. As foon as a fuitable

number

number of troops were inlifted, the great queftion refpected the fate of fuch of the rebels, as, after trial and conviction, were under fentence of death. On the one hand, to fuffer fuch high crimes as they had committed, to pafs away without punifhing the offenders, feemed to be fruftrating the ultimate defigns of juftice ; to be making the fituation of the guilty lefs ineligible than that of the innocent perfons who had fallen in the caufe of the country, and one of whom had been killed by a convict, whofe cafe was in queftion ; it feemed to be removing the great barriers which the laws had fet up for the prefervation of the body politick, by leffening the terrours annexed to the boldeft attempts upon its exiftence, in rendering the punifhment of offenders uncertain : The motives of mercy alfo, were liable to be mifconftrued by the party ftill in arms on the borders of the ftate, who, naturally defirous of increafing their confequence, would abfcribe that to a fear of their pitiful inroads and robberies, which would be the refult of infinitely fuperiour principles : This, inftead of introducing tranquillity, might lead them to attempts, which they would otherwife realize to be beyond their power. On the other hand, the low ftate of the rebellion, made fevere and fanguinary meafures lefs neceffary than ever to its extinction ; and to punifh,

when

when the evil was removed which it was the principal defign of the punifhment to remedy, would appear more like revenge in government, than the difpaffionate exercife of juftice. The convicts in queftion, though aggravatedly guilty, were not however, thofe leading characters which had moft attracted the publick attention; and if made examples, would excite a degree of pity in the minds of the people, from the obvious reflection that the lefs guilty were overtaken by the laws, while greater offenders efcaped unpunifhed. Above all, the faving of life was an object truly defirable, and to give place to nothing but the fafety of the Commonwealth.

UNDER fuch circumftances, the Supreme Executive determined upon a middle line of conduct; and on the 16th of *June* reprieved the convicts until the fecond of *Auguft* following; thereby retaining the fecurity which the government had, by the poffeffion of the prifoners, for the pacifick conduct of their affociates without the ftate, on the one hand; and avoiding furnifhing them with any new pretence for hoftilities, on the other. In the warrant of reprieve, the caufe of it was declared to be, the neceffity of further time, as well to difcover whether the lenient meafures adopted by the General Court, would have the happy confequences which they were intended to procure, as

to

to determine whether fpirited, decifive and forcible meafures would be neceffary to fupport the
government, and protect the citizens in that fecurity, which they were entitled to have under the
conftitution. A plain intimation to the malcontents, that their peaceable behaviour would fave
the lives of their brethren. At the fame time
that a reprieve was granted to the prifoners in
Hampfhire, the Sheriff of that county was ordered,
not to open his directions, until the criminals had
arrived at the gallows; by which means, the ufual preparations for the execution were attended
to, and the ability of the government to carry the
fentence into effect, fairly demonftrated.

THE reafons which operated to induce this reprieve, grew every day more influential; and were
thought fufficient to juftify a further reprieve, for
four of the convicts, to the 20th of *September*. A
full pardon was at length granted to a like number, among whom were *Parmenter* and *Shattuck*,
on the twelfth of the fame month. Of three who
were confined in the county of *Berkfhire*, two effected their efcape; and the other, who was convicted in *October*, was favoured with a commutation of his punifhment, to hard labour, for the
term of feven years.

THE military operations of the infurgents, during the fummer, were not of fufficient confequence
to

to be particularly mentioned, confifting rather of private robberies than publick hoftilities. So fecure was the ftate from any attacks on the 13th of *Auguft*, that the Governour reduced the troops to the number of 200. And on the twelfth day of *September* following, he had the high fatisfaction of announcing peace and tranquillity to the whole republick, by ordering the difcharge of all their forces.

IF any thing were wanting to complete the fuccefs of the meafures of government, with refpect to thofe deluded citizens who were concerned in the infurrections or rebellion, it was furnifhed from the voluntary conceffions of the criminals themfelves. The hardieft of them at length implored, with the moft humble contrition, the mercy which they had fo often rejected. Among others, *Shays* and *Parfons*, in the month of *February* 1788, preferred their petition to the late legiflature. In it they declared themfelves to be penetrated with a melancholy fenfe of their errours ; they averred their penitence, and plead the misfortunes to which they had been perfonally expofed, in the courfe of their unhappy oppofition to government, in expiation of their mifconduct. They gave affurances, that their future behaviour fhould evidence their fincerity. In extenuating, they wifhed not to appear to juftify their proceedings.

ings. They saw, they felt, and they owned that they had long felt the effects of their temerity, and they would never cease to regret their not having trusted for relief, to the wisdom and integrity of the ruling power. Whilst they acknowledged their errours, they entreated the legislature to believe, that these proceeded from misapprehension, and not from an abandoned principle. They had been obliged, they said, to seek an asylum far from their friends and connexions, in a state of exile from their country; yet, whatever had been suggested to the contrary, they had never combined with the secret enemies of *America*, if any such there were, to subvert her liberty or independence. If it should be thought necessary, that they should be held up as examples of suffering, to deter others, still enough had been done even for that purpose, as there was scarcely an inconvenience or misfortune which they could not number in their distresses. If these circumstances would not avail, they brought into view their friends, their wives and their children, who were innocent, and who, by their pardon, would be bound by new ties of gratitude and affection to the government : They declared that, in asking to be restored to their lost rights, they were not influenced by the fear of punishment, but by a wish to demonstrate the sincerity of their reformation,

mation, and to add to the inftances, already fo
confpicuous, of the clemency of the court.

A DISAGREEMENT in opinion between the two
houfes, prevented the legiflature from coming to
a decifion, upon this and many other fimilar petitions, which were before them. They were
therefore, of courfe, left for the confideration of
their fucceffours, who, on the 13th of *June* following, paffed a refolution, for juftifying all officers and öthers, who had apprehended fufpicious
perfons, who had ufed property, or who had entered into and quartered troops in houfes, in order to fupprefs the infurrections and rebellion, or
preferve the publick peace, or fafety of government; and for indemnifying all gaolers and fher-
iffs from whom prifoners had efcaped, or who had
been prevented ferving executions, by reafon of
the rebellion.

THIS conciliatory refolution alfo provided for
the indemnifying of all citizens who had been
concerned in the infurrections and rebellion, not
convicted thereof, except againft private fuits for
damages done to individuals, on condition of
their taking and fubfcribing the oath of allegiance
to the Commonwealth, within fix months after
the date ; and, with refpect to the nine perfons
excepted from the indemnity of the 13th of *June*
1787, on the further condition, that they fhould

never

never accept or hold any office, civil or military within the Commonwealth.

THUS was a dangerous internal war finally fuppreffed, by the fpirited ufe of conftitutional powers, without the fhedding of blood by the hand of the civil magiftrate; a circumftance, which it is the duty of every citizen to afcribe to its real caufe, the lenity of government, and not to their weaknefs; a circumftance too, that muft attach every man to a conftituion, which, from a happy principle of mediocrity, governs its fubjects without oppreffion, and reclaims them without feverity.

FINIS.

PRINTED AT *WORCESTER*, BY *ISAIAH THOMAS*, MDCCLXXXVIII.